Riddles of Life

Discovering and Harnessing Your Personal Power

Essays by
DEHNER A. FRANKS, SR.

Cover image © Jay Michaels

www.innovativeinkpublishing.com
Send all inquiries to:
4050 Westmark Drive
Dubuque, IA 52004-1840

Copyright © 2024 by Dehner A. Franks

Print ISBN: 979-8-3851-2667-5
eBook ISBN: 979-8-3851-2668-2

Published in the United States of America

Contents

Introduction

When I considered writing a new book I pondered what type of a book I would write. I decided to write short chapters which would deal with various aspects of daily living. I wanted to write a minimum of thirty one chapters, to allow the reader the option of reading one chapter per day, if desired. I have actually written more than thirty one chapters.

My life's path has been in no way traditional and because of the unique circumstances of my life, I have developed perspectives which may allow a fresh viewpoint.

I felt a need to write this after considering my life and some of the lessons I have learned through the "school of hard knocks" in a hope to encourage and inspire others.

This text, Riddles of Life, is a self-help book which focuses on many different aspects of daily living in an effort to enhance our lives and our relationships. The term "Riddles" lets us know that some things which are generally recognized one way, may have a deeper meaning upon a closer observation.

I have also introduced some of the concepts of universal laws, which are the foundation for everything in our lives. Everything and everyone in our lives are governed by universal laws and the more that we understand them, the more benefit we receive from this knowledge.

It is my desire in presenting this work to bring more joy, hope, happiness and love into the life of the reader and thereby make a small difference. It is remarkable the difference that just one person can make if we dare to step up, do our part and to let our voices be heard.

Over the past thirty plus years I have read many self-help books and literature on philosophy, the Bible and a broad array of information on recognizing and learning to utilize our personal power.

Growing up, my family moved a lot to many different parts of the country, which introduced me to many diverse experiences and has given me a broad perspective on life in general. I do not claim to be an authority on any of the ideas presented here, but I do feel qualified to share my views and to consolidate the information I have obtained within these pages.

I have included many references from people of great influence; including Presidents, celebrities, philosophers and many other significant individuals, to validate my views on various subjects.

As I began writing and sharing sections of this book with many different people, I consistently received positive feedback and the message that they were inspired by it and were anticipating it's release. Well, here it is! May you become inspired and empowered and perhaps even find your own answers as we uncover some of the *Riddles of Life!*

WHY A RIDDLE?

Humans find comfort in the predictable. We seek a world that is black and white. We like ready answers, fast food, easy fixes. The fact is that so much of what we believe to be true, may not actually be true after all.

Science has proven that, reduced down to the molecular level, all objects, which we perceive as solid objects, are composed mostly of space, with no particle touching another. In other words, the very ground we stand on is not solid ground after all.

The right side of our bodies are controlled by the left side of our brain, while the left side of our bodies are controlled by the right side of our brain, which definitely goes against our way of thinking. And many truths are being revealed in quantum physics, which stagger our minds with facts which are inconceivable to our way of reasoning.

And so it goes…

There are countless reversals in the world which defy our perceptions and are in many cases, counter to reason and logic.

So why a riddle? The idea of riddles as presented in this text refers to truths which may not be apparent upon first observation. For instance, through forgiving others we set ourselves free. So then, forgiveness is really a gift that we give to ourselves.

Many things in our lives are this way, appearing one way, while actually being another. Relying purely on appearances, then becomes insufficient and can cause us to perhaps miss some vital truths, hidden beneath the surface.

It is my endeavor in presenting this work, to attempt to uncover some hidden truths in everyday life, in an effort to empower and to bring greater understanding to the reader, in an effort to help us to discover a life of greater meaning and purpose.

Thank You!

I would like to thank the many people who have contributed to the development of this book. I have referenced several individuals, authors, celebrities, and others to support the ideas presented here.

Thank you to the many philosophers, authors and people whose words have inspired us through the years, with their speeches, teachings and writings, encouraging us to think on higher levels and to strive to become our very best.

I would like to thank my wife, Jan Dumain Franks for her insights, for her love and support. Jan is a writer herself and her wisdom and inspiration are of great value.

Thank you to Linné Girouard for her help with assisting me in obtaining and organizing reference material. Thank you to Amy Taylor for her help with the bibliography and for your friendship.

Thank you to Jay Michaels for his beautiful graphic design work and for his help, for his continued friendship and support.

Thank you to Innovative Ink, my publisher: to Angela Lampe and to Katie Celarek, whose contributions have made this publication possible. And thank you to Mike Moran for introducing me to my publisher.

Last, but not least, I thank God for the gift of life and for the many gifts that only He can bestow.

1

One of a Kind

The fact that every person is *one of a kind* carries with it tremendous implications. It means that we are not fated to the laws of conformity, nor to statistics, but we have within us the potential to become the exception to any and every rule; to become the first to accomplish any and every endeavor.

Because of our uniqueness and individuality, we are positioned to fulfill a destiny to which it seems we have been mysteriously crafted; perhaps predisposed, pre-selected??

How else to explain Michael Jordan (standing well over 6 feet tall with a physique designed perfectly for the sport) coming to the sport of basketball, dominating the game, discovering his destiny and making history? or a young Thomas Edison or Nicola Tesla finding their "knack" for inventing things (who collectively are responsible for well over fourteen hundred inventions), who go on to become two of the greatest inventors of all time, changing the world?

Not to mention the serendipitous circumstances of the perfect placement, historically, geographically, and the opportunities which produced such persons and innovators as Julius Caesar, William Shakespeare, Wolfgang Amadeus Mozart, Michelangelo, Leonardo, da Vinci, Abraham Lincoln, Saint Francis of Assisi, the Wright Brothers, Albert Einstein, the Dalai Lama, Martin Luther King, Jr, Theodore Roosevelt, Mahatma Gandhi, Mother Teresa, Princess Diana, Bill Gates, Steve Jobs, Barack Obama, Oprah Winfrey, Jeff Bezos, A. J.

Rollings, Elon Musk, YOU who are reading this, and the millions upon millions of those of us who have discovered our unique purposes and have literally changed the world!

On a personal level, my journey to becoming a professional pianist was not at all traditional, nor was it easy, yet it brought me to where I am today. When I began learning piano, I did not have piano lessons (I began taking formal piano lessons at age 19, four years after my initial stages of teaching myself to play), nor did I even have a piano at home.

I didn't read music very well and had many obstacles on my path to where I am today, yet somehow, I have found my place in the world; a destiny of which I am sure I was destined to find. Those things which appeared to be obstacles along the way, many of which have actually turned out to be assets in my approach to music.

So it is with each and every one of us. Though we dwell in a world of peers; on the job, at school, and in society among our friends and associates, still the truth remains that we are in a class all by ourselves. Each and every individual is truly one of a kind and we have the unique opportunity of defining and re-defining that person today and every day!

My uniqueness and individuality provide me a blank page, a canvas upon which to paint my life. My greatest gift is the gift of *myself* and as I become acquainted with myself, and share my uniqueness with the world, I will both find fulfillment and offer beauty to the world. Yes, I really am that special! *I am one of a kind!!*

2

Self-Validation

Oprah Winfrey stated, on the last show of her popular daytime television series:

"I've talked to nearly 30,000 people on this show, and all 30,000 had one thing in common — they all wanted validation. They wanted to know: Do you hear me? Do you see me? Does what I say mean anything to you?"

It is a fact that we all seek validation in life. It is a wonderful thing when we find people who are truly there for us; people we can count on. We all welcome the support of our friends and family.

Countless organizations all over the world have annual programs honoring its members with awards, and with warm words of support and appreciation for their dedication, outstanding service and contributions. Through our accomplishments we acquire confidence and receive validation.

However, sometimes we look to other people to cheer us on, and they are not around. To seek our validation solely from other people can become a handicap. What happens when the validation is not forthcoming? What about when we have to go through trials all alone, or when we have to deal with those who are against us or worse still, what about when people who were once for us, turn on us and are now against us? Then what?

In life there will be times when the only support available will be that which we give to ourselves. Self-validation is crucial to self-mastery and to personal development.

Though we may be alone and in need of support, we are not ever truly alone because we always have the company of ourselves. TV Host, Phillip C. McGraw, known more commonly as Dr. Phil stated,

"You're only lonely if you're not there for you."

Fortunately, there are things that we can do to bolster ourselves. The first step in self-validation is to recognize that, *"I matter!"* Then we can ask ourselves, "Why do I matter? How do I matter?" We can begin by assessing ourselves. Write a list of truths regarding yourself, an Asset List. For example:

<u>MY ASSETS</u>

1. Healthy
2. Happily employed
3. Have great friends/family
4. American citizen
5. Educated

We can list other assets such as: married, high school/college graduate, own my own business, etc.

We can also have a list of our outstanding character attributes:

1. Kind
2. Helpful
3. Witty
4. Strong
5. Courageous

These are just a few ideas to start off your Asset List. It is important to do regular self-assessments, because in life we are continually growing, changing and developing. Though we may feel the same, we are not the same person we were one year ago, or even last week!

Several years ago, I wrote a list of my individual assets and added to this list regularly. I went back later and counted over fifty entries on my list. Whenever I would read my asset list it would always give me a boost.

I also like to write affirmations, short statements affirming truths to myself, about myself to regularly assess where I am. Life should be a continuous journey of self-improvement.

Here's an example of one of my affirmations:

I am an encourager. I go out of my way to help and to empower people. I am kind and considerate. I work on myself daily, to become my very best. I am happy with who I am today, and I am excited about the person that I am becoming.

President Abraham Lincoln stated,

"I do not think much of a man who is not wiser today than he was yesterday."

That's quite a statement coming from a man, born in poverty, with an accumulative total time, in days, of *less than one year* of formal education his entire life, who rose to become the 16th President of the United States and is one of the most celebrated of all of the US Presidents. Lincoln was truly a self-made man, stating that everything he learned, he learned from reading books.

Self-validation is important, for every person we meet will have no higher opinion of us than we have of ourselves. The difference between "so-called" ordinary people and outstanding people is simply the latter's belief in themselves and their ability to sustain this belief with confidence. We really are all made of the same stuff.

One good technique I heard about is to practice looking in the mirror and talking to yourself. I would suggest that no one be around when you do this. You wouldn't want to give anyone the wrong impression. This practice may feel a little awkward at first but the more you practice it the more comfortable you'll feel and the more acquainted you'll become with yourself.

Look yourself in the eyes and say, "I love you." Then encourage yourself, affirming positive truths about yourself, to yourself; where you are now and where you're going in life, speaking to your reflection as you would your best friend. We really should have no better relationship in life, than our relationship with ourselves.

On the subject of self-improvement, here is a quote from Michelle Obama, former First Lady to President Barack Obama, from her book, "Becoming" as she mentions a practice of the former President Obama:

"To this day, when we arrive at a rental house in Hawaii or on Martha's Vineyard, Barack goes off looking for an empty room that can serve as the vacation hole. There, he can flip between the six or seven books he's reading simultaneously and toss his newspapers on the floor."

Wow, six or seven books and newspapers and he's not a student in school!

In her book she also mentions how Barack… *"read late into the night, often long after I'd fallen asleep, plowing through history and biographies and Toni Morrison, too. He read several newspapers daily, cover to cover."*

This is a clear example of someone who makes self-improvement a priority.

As we can see from the examples of President Lincoln and President Obama, and is true of countless others, is that to be successful we must maintain a *formula* for that success. Success doesn't just happen. Every successful person has a consistent formula for that success.

Here are a couple of valuable quotes from the success coach, Jim Rohn:

"Formal education will make you a living; self-education will make you a fortune."

"Success is nothing more than a few simple disciplines, practiced every day."

The more that we work on ourselves the stronger and more productive we become. So then, validation is not just something to affect other people's assessments of us, but it is also validating ourselves to ourselves. In essence, when we do the work, we can feel good about ourselves.

So, to summarize, validate yourself, believe in yourself and work to build yourself up on a daily basis. Adopt a program for belief in yourself and commit to a regular program of self-improvement.

Recognize your own worth and become your own greatest encourager and supporter. We, individually can make a difference in this world. We really can do and be above average. We can truly be exceptional!

3

Get Outdoors

Many people have lives so filled and so diverse that maintaining a balance can seem challenging. The monotony of going to work, day in and day out can be draining and leave us with little energy and vitality for anything else. Fortunately, there are things we can do to lighten the load.

Personally, I believe that there is an answer to any problem. Sometimes these answers are very simple and are right in front of us.

One answer to having renewed vitality and energy is a simple change of our routine, a change in the scenery. This shift can have a profound effect on our moods and can lift our spirits.

Recently, I spoke with a coworker who works indoors, in a room with no windows, and in an office with no windows and never gets outside during the course of her workday. I mentioned to her about the importance of getting outdoors.

If your job requires that you work indoors, that's fine. Perhaps on your breaks you could take a walk around the block and take in the beauty of the outdoors, or you may choose to eat lunch outside. Perhaps you could arrive to work a few minutes early to take a short walk before starting your day. This may seem like such a basic idea, but the effect of this practice has a real calming effect, plus the elements of exercise, a change of scenery and getting additional oxygen can't help but make us feel refreshed and renewed.

While we are enjoying the outdoors I would suggest being fully in the experience and not listening to music, not being lost in our thoughts or being on our cellphones, but rather enjoy the sights and sounds, listening to the rhythm of life.

Walk slowly, while taking in the beautiful sights, the designs of the greenery or flowers. Flowers are nature's testament to the beauty that is abundant all around us.

Smile at people as you pass them and appreciate the fashions and the smiles on their faces. Celebrate being alive. Enjoy all of the beauty that this life has to offer and recharge your batteries.

The more you let go and be "present" during this experience, the more you'll get out of it. One thing is for sure, if you practice this on a regular basis you will be happier and more centered. I know this from personal experience.

Additionally, take time to be outdoors on a regular basis. Just making a few small adjustments to our day can bring great rewards, relieve stress and help us to get more joy out of living.

4

Attitude

Sometimes optimists are labeled as idealists or are accused of having a "Pollyanna" perspective and are viewed in a negative light. The truth is that our disposition allows us a choice. We can choose to smile or frown; to laugh or not; to reach out or to withdraw our hands and our hearts. I live by a philosophy, "Choose to be happy."

Even when my life is not going well or I am hurting, just by taking my mind off of myself and shifting my view to helping someone else (who may be worse off than me), in so doing I immediately feel better. Yes, giving love is sometimes the greatest cure for our own troubles.

There is not a person living that has not had hurts, setbacks and problems along life's highway, though I'll admit that some, unfortunately, have had more bad breaks than others.

Whether we know it or not we each have a choice every day as to just how much of the burdens of life we choose to carry. What I mean by this is that our attitude plays a large part in the weight of our burdens. A bad attitude actually amplifies our burdens, making them seem much heavier. Even physical pain gains in intensity the more that we focus on it.

Our attitude, our disposition, can assist us in helping to relieve stress to a certain degree. A smile, extending a hand, being there for someone are all things that we can do to help in lifting our spirits while bringing joy to others.

Let's suppose that we were dealt a bad hand and feel a justification in our carrying a grudge, or a negative attitude. Yes, that which was done to us may have been unjust, but as we carry this grudge from day to day, now we are "coloring" *our own* future and *our* possibilities in shades of grey and the more that we carry this negative energy, and harbor animosity, the more of our own happiness and vital energy we are depleting and are negatively affecting both our present and our future. Negative states of mind react upon us and whether we realize it or not we ourselves will be the ones suffering from the results of a negative disposition, and not necessarily the person we are carrying the grudge against.

Try this approach, when faced with a problem, hurt, or setback, decide to regroup, center yourself, extend love to others and go again. Willfully shift your thoughts to positive, pleasant things and to the things that you love. If possible, get outdoors into nature and appreciate the beauty that is already abundantly flowing. Nature has a healing balm which can quickly shift our attention to something positive.

It is important to learn to set aside anything which is not beneficial to our journey and to our purpose. Is anything really worth sapping our strength, our happiness and spoiling our days? Let's not give our power away.

A negative, crabby attitude simply makes our burdens heavier, not to mention it pushes others away from us. Choose love, joy, peace and sharing and in time life will return to you of the good seeds that you have planted.

Yes, we can choose to be happy by extending love and good will. As someone once said, our *attitude* determines our *altitude*. One powerful tool for reducing stress is to physically relax your muscles. You can relax your shoulders, neck, arms, legs, etc. Do this while applying slow, deep breaths. This is an effective tool for quickly reducing stress.

The author, Norman Vincent Peale stated in his book, The Power of Positive Thinking,

"Attitudes are more important than facts."

That's quite a statement. Certainly worth pondering.

And this quote from Martha Washington, America's very first, First Lady and wife of George Washington, the first United States President, sums it up:

"I am still determined to be cheerful and happy, in whatever situation I may be; for I have also learned from experience that the greater part of our happiness or misery depends upon our dispositions, and not upon our circumstances." - Martha Washington

5

Labels

Whether we realize it or not, we all wear labels. Yes, everyone wears them and our lives are determined by them. Some labels are positive and useful while some are not. Sometimes we are not even aware of the things we are saying to ourselves, about ourselves.

Labels are attributes and characteristics regarding ourselves; the "truths" by which we define ourselves. Ironically, many of these labels are not true at all, but rather are things which we have *accepted* as true.

For instance, perhaps someone may once have called us a "mean and uncaring person" and we may have unconsciously accepted this as true, when in reality perhaps it never was true. As we have accepted this belief, now it is affecting all of our relationships. This can cast a shadow over us, affecting our behavior and negatively affect our belief in ourselves.

Our self-image is the foundation of the person *we believe ourselves to be,* and this determines the very parameters of everything in our lives. Labels are incorporated into this self-image on a subconscious level.

We define ourselves based on a wide variety of parameters: information told us by our parents, siblings, teachers, our spouse, friends, enemies, business associates; things we have told ourselves; things we have read, and a host of other sources. Also included in this list are beliefs based on social beliefs and biases. Needless to say, much of this information is fragmented, outdated, distorted and inaccurate.

Over time these ideas are assimilated into our psyche and become a part of our "blueprint" or the basis of the ideas which we use to define who we are as an individual. Acceptance of these ideas determines our self-image, the person that we *believe* ourselves to be.

We need to be discerning about what we accept as "true" regarding ourselves, as the acceptance of false beliefs and negative labels can be devastating to our egos and to our lives.

When a negative label is identified within us, refuse to wear the label. For instance, someone may call you a bad name or may call you incompetent. Whether or not we wear the label is entirely our choice. Even if you agree that you have a weakness in a particular area, yes, you may accept this as a fact, but to wear a negative label keeps you confined to the limits of the label.

Refuse to wear any labels that are not beneficial and that you do not agree with. Yes, we can all recognize areas that we need to work on, but it is *our* responsibility to take care of these issues, not someone else's.

Some people accept a negative label and wear it their entire lives and are stunted by this acceptance. It is a good practice to evaluate the beliefs we have about ourselves and to construct a positive program of self-awareness and self-improvement which allows us to feel good about ourselves and which aids us in accomplishing our very best.

Yes, we all have some negative qualities and a few shortcomings which we need to acknowledge. But acknowledgement is not the same thing as acceptance and certainly not the same as a self-definition.

To say that "I have failed" may be accurate. To say that "I am a failure" is to adopt a negative label which is a mislabeling of ourselves. To acknowledge oneself as a failure is to undermine ourselves at every turn. Never build a case against yourself.

The Irish poet and playwright, Oscar Wilde stated,

Most people are other people. Their thoughts are someone else's opinions, their lives a mimicry, their passions a quotation.

Some people carry the guilt and shame of labels which were placed upon them, that were never the truth or were based on something that took place many years ago. Perhaps someone perceived something a certain way, and then proceeded to place accusation and blame which was never founded on the truth.

Sometimes people are accused of malicious acts, when in some cases the acts were not malicious at all but were misinterpreted.

Unfortunately, many people carry the guilt and shame of burdens which are outdated or were never true. The effects of carrying such burdens are just as destructive as if they were the truth. Whatever we "own" becomes our truth. Stop carrying burdens that other people foist upon us. If we know in our hearts it's not the truth, or that the intention was not malicious, then stop acting as if it were true and let go of that negative baggage.

This happens a lot with outdated matters from our past. Even if we are guilty of an offense, if its not productive nor relevant to our lives today, then discard the label. Such an acceptance of negativity will cripple our lives.

None of us are the same person we were 5, 10 or 20 years ago. Stop re-hashing the past. Just like food with an expired label, if its out of date, throw it away!!

Additionally, we put labels on every person in our lives. This determines how we interact with others and is an unconscious basis of all of our relationships.

When we meet someone, we automatically assess the individual and our "like" or "dislike" of them. Unconsciously we place our labels on them. I discovered something amazing in my dealings with people. I have had a number of incidents where *re-labeling* has been the avenue of changing negative relationships into positive ones.

For example, if we are experiencing negativity in a relationship, it might be a good idea to evaluate just what *we* are feeling regarding the other person and perhaps re-label or change what we are saying to ourselves about the people in our lives.

Through re-labeling, we automatically *change* our feelings and our interactions with these individuals, which changes the situation or relationship, according to the label or the "name" that we give them. This is one of the riddles of life.

I have had instances where I had experienced negativity from certain people over an extended period of time, and then after re-labeling and renaming the situation, my interactions with them changed, turning the negativity into positive relationships, according to the nature of my positive statements regarding them. The relationship *reflected* back to me the new label, or the new name that I had placed on it!

This concept operates the same way that positive affirmation works in helping us in changing our own behaviors. The difference is that now we are speaking positive affirmations regarding other people. Give it a try. I think you'll find this as amazing as I have found it to be.

To summarize, drop the negative labels and replace them with badges of honor. We should learn to define ourselves and others by the labels of love, goodness and that which builds up and encourages. If a label regarding yourself or others is not beneficial, you need to discard it and replace it with one that is positive and life-giving.

6

What Gifts!

How wonderful I am. How amazing my lot in life. How beautiful this life. With my eyes I behold glorious sunsets and, in the morning, the enchanting waking of the sun. The scene is picturesque; this glorious, wonderful world.

Sometimes I watch the squirrels as they scamper through the grass, playing their delightful games, or suddenly stand still, breathless, captivated by a glimpse of nature's entrancing artistry. I am immersed in beauty all around. What a gift, I can see!! Sometimes I forget just how full my cup, or how amazing is my life.

I take a walk and gaze upon the flowers along the way. Funny, I hadn't noticed them there before. They fill the air with fragrant delight and show off their exquisite colors and designs.

I can hear so many songs of birds, singing in the trees and feel their joy in living. As I take it all in, my soul is filled and I am again renewed.

Sometimes I listen to my favorite songs and break into a dance, swaying to the beat. Other times I listen to the waves upon the beach or to the distinct voices of those I love and realize, what a gift this is, I can hear!!

While leafing through my photos I am reminded of all the places I've been. So many delights, loves, joys and adventures. Then I see that perhaps I need to slow down and take it all in. Take the time to smell the roses along the way.

Even the rains of life are as the showers in the field, but for a purpose; to bring forth a greater harvest through cleansing and nourishing the earth.

Yes, this really is an amazing life and as I take my mind away from being in my head, but rather behold the beauty that is all around, I have to smile and be glad for what was, for what is and for what is to come.

We are fortunate to be a part of this life. What a gift, I am alive!! I will take in this moment; savor it, nurture it and be glad for it and celebrate these gifts. I will celebrate this beautiful, wonderful world, this wonderful life!!

7

The Clock on the Wall

Iregularly have lunch with a fellow pianist, a friend of mine, who would often comment about his age. He is in his eighties and would often speak of being old. Whenever we would talk, it was as though he were watching the clock on the wall, waiting for his impending demise.

I reminded my friend that our purpose in being here in the land of the living is not to sit and stare at the clock on the wall, so to speak, but rather to be busy living, doing and fulfilling our purpose and ignoring the time. I said to him, "What if you lived to be one hundred, or beyond, as many people are today, are you going to squander the next 20 years staring at the clock on the wall?"

One thing is for certain if we begin to ponder our demise we may hasten it, for we tend to get what we consistently think on. We attract to ourselves the things that we anticipate or expect, whether they are beneficial or not. We'll discuss more on this later.

Fortunately, I still meet with this friend and our conversations have changed. He has become inspired about living and is focused more on living life in this present moment, rather than keeping his thoughts fixed on the future.

I reminded my friend of a former piano teacher I studied with, Mary Toy, of Kirkland, Washington, who is presently around one hundred years old and who is always vibrant and full of life. Her sister just passed a couple of months ago at age 104!

Mary told me that one of her piano students asked her about the secret of her and her sister's longevity. She mentioned to him, her faith in God, keeping active and being around young people, as many of her piano students are young.

Mary is such an inspiration to me and to many. I began studying piano with her when she was in her mid-eighties, and she was very active in music at that time, even taking a trip from Washington State to study in Russia to learn a new piano teaching style. She never even noticed her age, as she was so busy with living and making a difference.

In an article from the Spokesman Review entitled, Teacher of Generations, Mary is quoted as saying,

> *"Age means nothing," she said. "Life is how you live, embrace and react to it all."*

She is an amazing person and by far the best Classical piano teacher I have ever studied with and has always been one of the most positive and inspiring people I've ever known. I'm convinced that her attitude also plays a major role in her health, happiness and longevity.

In the book, Ageless Body, Timeless Mind by Deepak Chopra, he talks about communities of centenarians all over the world, where a large number of the people are either approaching or have exceeded the one-hundred-year-old mark.

In the book he presents the idea that our bodies begin to break down as a result of our society's emphasis on statistics of age limits and so forth. We are literally "taught" here, in our society, what sicknesses we are to *expect* at a certain age and of the limits of our life expectancy. Many people accept these statistics as "Gospel" and anticipate their negative results.

Here is a statistic dated January 9, 2024, by Katherine Schaeffer, a research analyst at Pew Research Center:

> *"The number of Americans ages 100 and older is projected to more than quadruple over the next three decades, from an estimated 101,000 in 2024 to about 422,000 in 2054, according to projections from the U.S. Census Bureau."*

Some major factors and common denominators among these centenarians are of course their attitudes, diets and their lifestyles. Another key component among them is maintaining a strong support base from friends and family.

In the Deepak Chopra book, Ageless Body, Timeless Mind, he emphasizes the connection between mind and body responses.

"Medicine is just beginning to use the mind-body connection for healing- defeating pain is a good example. By giving a placebo, or dummy, drug, 30 percent of patients will experience the same pain relief as if a real painkiller had been administered."

Imagine that, receiving actual results from a dummy pill! This presents very real evidence of the power of the mind, the power of belief. Chopra continues…

"But the mind-body effect is much more holistic. The same dummy pill can be used to kill pain, to stop excessive gastric secretions in ulcer patients, to lower blood pressure, or to fight tumors."

I would like to add here that I am not a medical doctor, nor am I advising anyone to pursue any avenues which are not supported by sound, professional, medical advice. If a person is experiencing a medical condition I suggest seeking qualified medical attention.

I am simply conveying the fact, as is supposed and is well documented in medical practice, that our minds, our thoughts and our expectations play a vital role in the state of our health, which can affect us, both positively and negatively. Here is another interesting thought from this same book:

"Because the mind influences every cell in the body, human aging is fluid and changeable; it can speed up, slow down, stop for a time, and even reverse itself."

He goes on to say…

"Hundreds of research findings from the last three decades have verified that aging is much more dependent on the individual than was ever dreamed of in the past."

As presented here in this text, when we take our focus off of our society's tendencies to predetermined age limits and anticipated illnesses and the negative effects of aging, but rather focus on the things that tend to life, it actually halts this negative progression, for everything that we are and everything that we do come from our thoughts, for better or for worse.

Currently there is a Netflix series, Live to 100: Secrets of the Blue Zones documentary which again, highlights various regions around the world with high concentrations of centenarians, or persons approaching and those exceeding the one-hundred-year-old mark. So, then the thought of living to be one hundred years old or beyond is not at all improbable.

Here's another thought while we're on the subject of longevity, we've all heard the phrase, "bucket list", which of course refers to the things we want to accomplish before we die, or as the old saying goes, before we "Kick the bucket." In fact, there is a movie of this same title which has made it a common phrase in our society. The use of this term, "bucket list" is seen as *en vogue* and people say it without giving it a second thought.

Our words have tremendous power. I don't think that we realize just how much power is in our words. Because of this fact, I think that we need to be careful of the things that we speak, for our words have power to bring about our reality.

When we say that we are accomplishing things on our "bucket list", have we considered that with the completion of every item on the list we are laying out the steps, or the pathway to our end? We may not realize it, but in creating this list and checking off the completed events, *we* have defined the steps which have started a clock, a countdown of a list, the completion of which marks… the end of our life.

The more of the things we accomplish from our bucket list, puts us one step closer to the end of the list and of course we know what happens at the end of the list. From this perspective we can see it as a trap, a web of our own making.

I have decided not to use the phrase "bucket list", but rather I say something like, my goals, or things that I plan to accomplish, in my lifetime. This way I'm not telling myself to start a countdown, but I'm simply living my life on my own terms, and enjoying the journey, every step of the way.

While I'm in the land of the living I'll focus on living, laughing, loving and fulfilling my purpose and my purpose is too important for me to be distracted by counting down my time here or to sit around, staring at the clock on the wall.

8

We Need Each Other

My sister Nancy once told me that our Maker would not have made so many billions of people on this planet if we were supposed to be alone. How true.

I confess that I don't have all of the answers and this makes me see the value in listening to other people. My father used to say how important it is to listen to anyone, to respect other people's opinions and he stressed that everyone has value.

Taking time to listen to others is a gift that we give to them. Sometimes it's best not to speak at all, but to take a genuine interest in listening to other people. Become a sounding board. You will bring joy to others the more that you exercise this and you will be pleasantly surprised to learn something new.

Albert Einstein, one of the greatest geniuses of all time said,

"You cannot solve a problem with the same mind that created it."

According to this statement then, we really do need each other!

Mankind's greatness is brought about through our collective wisdom, our collective understanding and our collective experiences. The vast majority of humanity's inventions and breakthroughs have been the result of the work of individuals who have gone ahead of the ones who were recognized for the discovery, paving the way, and then the breakthrough came as a result of other people adding to these previous findings.

I enjoy reading books and have discovered that I might only get one sentence or one phrase from an author, which I can add to other phrases from other authors and thereby gain greater understanding on a certain subject. No one person has all the answers.

Steve Jobs, the founder of the phenomenally successful Apple Technology Company made the statement,

"It doesn't make sense to hire smart people and then tell them what to do; we hire smart people so they can tell us what to do." – Steve Jobs.

There is much wisdom in this philosophy and Apple's success certainly tells the story and supports the fact that we are stronger, together.

This is why holding prejudices towards groups of people is counterproductive. The person harboring this negative view is simply limiting their own possibilities and are coloring their own hearts in shades of grey.

Racial prejudice is even more limiting when we understand that now we are negating multi-millions of people, the majority of which we have and never will meet and have disregarded, based on our own personal biases, or because of a need to hold to such beliefs in order to be accepted by a certain group. Anything that requires us to act a certain way or which demands that we conform to ideals which may not necessarily be our own, is counterproductive to peace, harmony and personal autonomy.

In the negating of an entire segment of the earth's population we are simply cutting ourselves off from infinite possibilities, opportunities, joys, creativity, love, insights and the beauty that's only to be found in the beauty of an individual and in our diversity.

Interestingly, our treasure, or the answers we are seeking may be discovered in an unexpected place or hidden within the heart, mind or soul of the most unlikely of vessels, perhaps even hidden among those of which we have so distanced ourselves. There is an old, wise saying, "Never burn a bridge, as you never know when you may need to cross over it at some point in time." Never throw away a person.

The worth of a human being cannot be measured by any finite terms. Yes, each of us really is that special. We are all a part of life's tapestry; each part necessary, intricately woven together into the whole.

This brings us to the subject of love and relationships. This is one of the broadest of topics, which cannot be sufficiently discussed here. However, I would like to mention a couple of points.

There is much talk in the world about love. So often we define love by our feelings. Yes, love is often accompanied by warm feelings, but love is more than just a feeling.

The English language uses one word for love which limits our ability to sufficiently communicate our feelings or intent. To say that "I love you." and in the next sentence say, "I love hotdogs." is certainly not sufficient.

The Greek language, however, has many different words for the different kinds of love. Here are four Greek words for love: Philia, represents love in friendship and affection, Storge is used in referring to love in family relationships, Eros, denotes romantic love and Agape love is unconditional, sacrificial love. This is the word used in describing Divine love.

Agape love is the highest form of love. It does not say, "I love you *for what* you are." but rather, "I love you *because* you are." This is pure love, that is not based on what a person does or does not do, nor is it based on any outside parameters.

The closest we can come to pure agape love is to offer love without conditions. Such a love says, "I love you *as* you are: *where* you are, *how* you are and for *who* you are." Making the conscious decision to overlook faults and deficiencies, we make love a choice, which says, "I *choose* to love you, unconditionally."

Love encompasses our intimate relationships as well as our friendships. Friendships are a vital part of life and to navigate them successfully is to bring greater joy and greater meaning to our lives.

Here is a beautiful quote by Abraham Lincoln,

> *"Every man is said to have his peculiar ambition ... I have no other so great as that of being truly esteemed of my fellow men, by rendering myself worthy of their esteem."*

In essence, to have friends, be a friend. In a good relationship, sharing is a vital factor. It is good to put actions behind our words. There is a saying,

"Actions speak louder than words." There are friendships and then there are acquaintances. There is a term, a "fair-weather-friend", which of course speaks of the "friends" who are around when everything is going well, but are not to be found during periods of difficulty.

These types of acquaintances cannot be called friendships. My sister Leona has a phrase which speaks to these kinds of "friends", which goes like this, "I'm your friend through thick and thin. When things get too thick, I thin out!" These are not the kind of friends I'm referring to.

One-sided relationships are not healthy ones. Relationships must be mutually beneficial to be considered a healthy relationship. If both parties are not adequately benefiting from the relationship, then I would question whether or not it's a healthy relationship and if it's not properly balanced, then perhaps we may want to question continuing the relationship.

Our focus in our interpersonal relationships should never be solely on receiving, but our focus should be on giving to the relationship. If both parties are focused on giving to each other, then the receiving will take care of itself, but if your focus is on receiving, then you are facing in the wrong direction.

We can think of our relationships as a garden, which must be cultivated that it might flourish and bring forth fruit. It is a good idea to contact anyone you feel as important in your life on a regular basis, otherwise your garden (your friends and family) will be overrun with "weeds" (assumptions as to why you haven't kept in touch), and your "harvest" (your relationships), will not flourish.

Relationships must be nurtured to thrive. Regular visits, phone calls, texting, sending cards and letter writing are all ways we can tend to our garden of friends and loved ones.

On the subject of texting and phone calls, it is a good practice to get right back to people in a timely manner. To wait for long periods of time before returning a text or a phone call sends a bad message, which is, in essence saying, "You're not important enough for me to respond to you in a timely manner." My advice is to try your best to treat *every* person with the same respect, as you would like to be treated.

To enjoy beauty in relationships, nurture them and don't take people for granted and you will enjoy one of life's greatest treasures, the gift of love through expressing the beauty of caring, sharing and enjoying mutual love and fellowship.

9

Normal

I once had someone tell me that what we call normal behavior is entirely subjective. He asked the question, "What is normal?" He stated that "Everyone is a little 'off' in one way or another." In addressing this generalized statement we have to first ask the question, by whose standards are we classifying what we call normal?

I think that this is an important question because some people may have defined themselves in a negative light, perhaps even as abnormal, when perhaps they are no less "normal" than anyone else. It is certain that every human being has deficiencies in one area or another.

Perhaps someone may not be good at sports, but is an excellent mathematician, or perhaps another person is deficient in speech, but is an outstanding engineer. Another may be outstanding athletically but deficient in social skills.

The point is that we all have strengths and weaknesses, but we are all capable human beings. It is when we get into the area of competing with others that we may fall short, because we sometimes try to gage ourselves based on another person's criteria which may be foreign to us, certainly not our own.

Yes, we may fall short because we are all unique and individual. One thing is for certain, no one can be *me* any better than *I* can be *myself!*

Let's deviate for a moment…. Let's consider all of the heroes of our wonderful children's stories which tell of the one beating the odds and going on to accomplish great things.

What about the story of Rudolph the Red-Nosed Reindeer, or of the Ugly Duckling, A Bug's Life, or of Belle, in Beauty and the Beast, or Finding Nemo, the stories of those who just didn't fit in? There are countless stories, allegories to real life situations whose very message is in the triumph of the one that was seen as "abnormal", the one who just didn't fit the norm, who became the hero of the story. What would the story of Rudolph the Red-Nosed Reindeer be without Rudolph?

Looking beyond the subject of children's stories and of what classifies as "normal", let's look at real-life accomplishments of those who were said to be deficient, as insufficient to the task. Many of the greatest achievements in history have come about by those who were told they could not achieve their desired goals.

In 1942 a British mathematician, considered to be a social misfit, Alan Turing, was told repeatedly that he would fail in his venture; however, he was successful in helping to create a machine which would crack Nazi Germany's Enigma code, which provided vital intelligence to the resistance, hastening the end to WWII. Additionally, Turing's invention laid the groundwork for modern computing.

Steven Hawking, a paraplegic, was an English theoretical physicist, cosmologist, and author who, at the time of his death, was director of research at the Centre for Theoretical Cosmology at the University of Cambridge, whose breakthrough discovery has made the detailed study of black holes possible.

The Wright Brothers were bicycle builders, who were considered to be crazy, believing that man could fly, who eventually succeeded in the invention of the airplane, making their first successful flight in 1903, ushering in the age of aviation.

A more recent example is the phenomenally successful motivational speaker, Les Brown, who as a child was told that he was retarded. Instead of his accepting this presumption, he rejected the labels and has become overwhelmingly successful, winning many awards and is in high demand for his dynamic skill as a speaker and motivator. Les Brown, speaking from experience, stated,

"Don't let someone else's opinion of you become your reality."

Overcoming the odds is one indication that listening to what "they" say is not necessarily a sound foundation on which to build our lives. So, what "they" say about normal is not necessarily normal. So many people who were told that they could not, did, and every day another tale of what couldn't be done is being overturned.

So then, perhaps our version of "normal" might be a way of maintaining a certain status quo, but history is full of the exceptions; those that dared to dream and defied the odds.

In considering those considered as abnormal, we shouldn't be too quick to judge. Obviously observing the basic rule of treating others with respect is a basic rule of society which we need to keep in place. If a person's eccentric behavior violates another person, this is not acceptable. But perhaps we can celebrate our differences and instead of feeling inadequate, that we are not as "everybody else" (which is a rash generalization, as there is no standard, nor ideal person), to turn that around and to realize that perhaps we are just as we are for a greater purpose. Perhaps our unique qualities, as in the case of Rudolph, may even turn out to be our greatest asset.

10

By Chance or by Law?

There are many things in life that we attribute to chance, which may actually be the result of universal laws. First, we need to understand that there are many laws of nature, which govern our world.

Take gravity for example; the natural force which attracts everything down toward the center of the earth. Here is a natural law, which we can use to our advantage, or conversely, we will have a negative result when we try to deny it or to refute its validity. The law of gravity, as with all natural laws, does not deviate, only being operational occasionally; Oh no, these laws of the universe are always in operation and are as consistent as the law of gravity.

There is a law of *seed time and harvest,* which brings forth food from the earth in its proper season, sustaining life on earth and has done so consistently for countless centuries, since the dawn of mankind.

There is a law of *cause and effect;* and to every effect there is a cause. Every action causes a spontaneous reaction. This law is operational on all levels of life: on a chemical, molecular, mental and on a physical level. Nothing happens, "Just because..." Issac Newton's third law of motion published in 1687, supports this in his findings, simply stating that,

For every action there is an equal and opposite reaction.

There is a law of *vibration*. Everything is energy and is in constant vibration. The atom is the smallest known particle, which is constantly in motion, in vibration. This law of vibration touches everything we know on both the material and even on non-material levels.

There is a law of *sowing and reaping,* or in some disciplines this law may be referred to as *karma*. This law states that the things that we do today will have future repercussions or consequences, depending on the type of deeds done or the "seeds" planted.

Many philosophers teach about the correlation between the events of our lives and the thoughts which we habitually possess. According to this philosophy, the conclusion is that outward events had their beginnings in the realm of thoughts and later manifested in the material world.

The law of *attraction,* is one such law, based on the mind's workings; like a magnet attracting, the things we think on, bringing into the material world, things like itself. This law states that what we think about on a habitual basis, we attract to ourselves, whether it is beneficial or not. A common phrase is, "a self-fulfilling prophecy", which is indicative of this law.

The significance of such a concept, would then make it imperative that we make sure that we are thinking healthy thoughts, so as not to contribute to the production of undesirable conditions.

The law of *assumption* is a powerful law which demonstrates the power of belief. In the operation of this law an individual can propel oneself to a higher state of living by *assuming* the desired state in the present. This law becomes operative through the sense of *feeling* and *imagining* oneself already being, living and operating in the state of the wish fulfilled.

The great physicist, Albert Einstein made a statement which validates such a law,

> *"Everything is energy and that's all there is to it. Match the frequency of the reality you want and you can't help but get that reality. It can be no other way. This is not philosophy, this is physics."*

There is a law of *faith*. The Bible is filled with references to faith, or the law of faith, which states that,

With God all things are possible.

It further states that,

The things which are impossible with men, are possible with God.

and

Whatsoever things you desire, when you pray, believe that you receive them, and you shall have them.

The world is filled with countless testimonies of things which seemed impossible, that were accomplished through a sustained faith. There are an innumerable number of documented cases of miraculous recovery from a plethora of diverse situations, defying medicine, science and logic, with the only answer being the successful application of the law of faith.

This brings us to an interesting point. The worlds of science, philosophy and religion are all based on the premise of truth, though it is obvious that not all doctrines, theories and ideologies are necessarily true. There is much dissension among people surrounding each of these areas.

If indeed the particular religion, science or philosophy is *actually* true, there would be no need for division, for truth is harmonious with itself and with life. Truth needs no defending. Truth is just truth!

The arguments of science against religion are unnecessary, if both are indeed true. Science, then would actually compliment the religious teachings and vice a verse, as is the case upon closer observation.

It is important to understand that in dealing with the laws of the universe, our positioning, relative to the law, is vital. The law can work *for* us or *against* us depending upon our positioning. Everything and everyone in the world is continually under the jurisdiction of these laws, as these are not temporal laws, but universal and eternal.

Consider this, the imagination plays an important role in the events of our lives. An interesting thing about the imagination is that it cannot tell the difference between a vividly imagined image and reality. This is why our dreams during sleep are so vivid and real to us, and then we awaken, only to discover that it was just a dream.

While it is true that the imagination is infinitely creative and that all human inventions began in the imagination, it is important to understand that this faculty works both actively and passively.

Let's consider the issue of positioning in relationship to universal laws and of the imagination. These laws work just as effectively in producing both negative and positive results.

There is a well-known Bible story of a man named Job, who went through a season of tremendous loss and great suffering. When we look further at his story, we discover, through his own words, how this was brought about. Job made the definitive statement in the words,

"The thing that I feared the most has come upon me."

Through this statement and with the understanding of the force of attraction, we can clearly see that it was his great fear of dreaded events, purely imagined, which actually attracted his calamity to himself.

Or for something more current, in 1995, the actor Christopher Reeve was cast in a movie, Above Suspicion, playing the part of a paralyzed man in the movie. A short time later he was involved in an accident at an equestrian event which actually rendered him paralyzed. The part he played in the movie became his reality.

Or, on November 30, 2013, in another twist of fate, Paul Walker, the star of a popular movie, The Fast and the Furious perished in a fiery car crash while still filming the movie, The Fast and the Furious 7, a movie about high-speed chases and car crashes. Coincidences? I would have to consider that perhaps there's a little more to it, especially when I look back over my own life and discover many events, which upon observation, directly correlated to my thinking at the time.

Again, a most important fact about the imagination is that it cannot tell the difference between actual facts or a vividly imagined image. It is for this reason I think that it is imperative that we take moments in our day to "clear the slate" through practicing silence as a means of clearing our inner thoughts.

Next, we can begin to replace the negative thoughts with positive ones. Through *thought conditioning* we can cancel out negative thought patterns and instead, use our imaginations to attract the things that we would want to show up in our lives.

Now for the good news, the fact is that the imagination can also become a tool for amazing, beautiful things as well. As our thoughts, words and feelings align with positive outcomes, vividly imagined, they too become our present realities, manifesting infinite possibilities.

Such individuals as Steve Jobs, Oprah Winfrey, Tyler Perry, Elon Musk, J.K. Rowling, Jim Carey and countless others have openly shared their stories as testaments to the power of the imagination as a tool of infinite goodness and amazing success.

I would like to point out that all of the laws governing the universe and the imagination are neutral. There is nothing evil about our imagination nor any of these laws, nor is any person *fated* to experience their negative effects. *We* are the ones who decide the effects of these laws upon our lives according to the way that we align with these laws, through the type of thoughts that we habitually entertain. The results in our lives are based on our vantage point.

A good analogy for the use of these powers can be seen in the power of electricity. Electricity is a power that we use for multiple positive uses for great benefit. The use of electricity in the world is universal and is enormously beneficial. We, as a society, have come to depend on this essential energy source.

Conversely this power can be destructive, even detrimental, if we use it improperly. So it is with all of these laws.

It is for this reason that it is important for people who work as counselors, actors, trauma care workers, ministers, those in law enforcement, medical personnel, social workers and those who deal with people's problems on a regular basis, have regular methods of catharsis, practices for "reprogramming" their minds and their imaginations to positive thoughts and feelings.

Many people have little to no awareness of any such universal laws, relying solely on the material world and the five physical senses. Believing in chance for some may seem "safe", as in the saying, "ignorance is bliss."

Perhaps a refusal to accept a concept outside of our natural understanding may provide a sort of way of playing it "safe", but in embracing the truth of the proven scientific facts of these laws, allows us to perhaps have more of a say than we realize in how our lives turn out, giving us a hand in the shaping of our destinies and can aid us in our lifetime pursuits.

For those who may have difficulty understanding the reality of these laws and their operation, may perhaps use our understanding of wireless technology as a model.

It is inconceivable that on any given day, billions of phone conversations are transmitted simultaneously through the various mediums of wireless communication. Just how we are able to send documents to the other side of the world in a matter of seconds, accurately pinpointing its destination is inconceivable.

We can transmit conversations, books, photographs, images, movies and a long list of media through processes which we cannot fully comprehend, yet the physical evidence proves this capability. So it is with these universal laws. We may not fully understand the processes through which they operate but the evidence of their power is undeniable.

Here are a few quotes on this subject:

"Our life is what our thoughts make it." - Marcus Aurelius, Roman Emperor

*"Once you make a decision, the universe conspires to make it happen."
- Ralph Waldo Emerson, Greek Philosopher*

"Where focus goes, energy flows. And where energy flows, whatever you're focusing on grows. In other words, your life is controlled by what you focus on. That's why you need to focus on where you want to go, not on what you fear." - Tony Robbins, Motivational Speaker

"If you want to find the secrets of the Universe, think in terms of energy, frequency, and vibration." - Nicola Tesla, Inventor

"The state of your life is nothing more than a reflection of your state of mind." - Wayne Dyer, Author

*"You get in life what you have the courage to ask for.
You don't become what you want, you become what you believe."
- Oprah Winfrey, TV Host*

Is it by chance or by law? You be the judge.

11

Letting Ourselves Off the Hook

We all make mistakes in life and we all have regrets for some of our choices. There's no getting around it, life can be challenging.

The important thing in life is not so much *what* we go through, but it's *how* we go through it that matters. Some people come through opposition, setbacks, failures and humiliations and come out stronger while others are crushed under a burden of failures, disappointments and regrets.

To begin with we need to make sure that we're not beating ourselves up for our mistakes, because as with us all; the one person that I will have to deal with for my entire life is myself.

This is not to say that we don't need to own our part in our mess-ups. We need to do all that we can to be honest, ethical and to have forgiveness and empathy both for ourselves and for others. But after we have apologized for our mistakes and done all that we can do to make amends, accepting the consequences of our actions, now we need to put the past behind us and focus on moving forward. Don't beat yourself up repeatedly. Drop it and move on.

Many people become stuck in regret, guilt and self-pity, unable to move forward. Such a mentality can be self destructive, as we seek to find reconciliation, through using denial of our own happiness as a form of penance, which is futile, as it is not possible to *undo* the mistakes of the past.

Understandably, after making a mistake, there will be a period of regret and perhaps even self-condemnation. This is normal. It is important to learn whatever lessons we need to learn from our mistakes.

It is when this self-loathing and regret becomes habitual that it can begin to create bigger problems. It is important to know when it is time to get over it and to move on.

Some people become vindictive and strike out at others and in so doing create more problems. Certainly, this is not the best path. The choices we make at these times of uncertainty are vitally important and must be made from a standpoint of a clear mind; with empathy, forgiveness and understanding for ourselves and for all involved.

All of our life lies before us. That which lays behind us cannot be repeated. The only thing we can do with the past is to learn from it and then leave it in the past.

In the Disney movie, A Far Off Place, a movie about the tragic effects of a family caught in the crossfire of evil ivory poachers, tells the story of the only survivors, two young children, who struggle to survive as they travel through the harsh Kalahari Desert to escape. Their only help comes from an African Bushman, Xhabbo, who leads them on a long, arduous journey to their freedom.

At the end of their ordeal, while considering the tragedy and loss these two young children have endured, Xhabbo gives them these final words of wisdom, *"Don't look back."*, as they part ways. This is a good philosophy to live by.

Our peace and our purpose abide, in this present moment, not in our past. No matter how big a situation or how much regret we may have for past events, there is only *now*, this present moment, that we can do anything about.

This moment allows us a choice, our only choice, to live in freedom or to live in the sorrows and regrets of the past. There is a peace that comes from inhabiting our moments, one moment at a time.

It is equally important not to succumb to the trap of wallowing in self-pity. No, things didn't go as planned; yes, perhaps this was a mistake; yes, I feel bad about it, but if after seeking every avenue to rectify the situation and find that there's nothing we can do to change it, then the only choice is to just drop it.

If we can do something to make amends, by all means do so, but don't wallow over your mistakes. Self-pity can lead to worse states of feeling unworthy, preventing us from moving forward. Some individuals become trapped in this mindset while some unfortunate individuals may remain stuck for the rest of their lives.

Some others go so far as to try to punish themselves in some way for their mistakes. Such actions are futile and only produce more problems. As I said before, the best thing we can do with the past is to learn from it and seek to do better in the future.

We may have to live with a few regrets for some of our life choices, but *"What about today?"* This is the question we need to ask ourselves, because today is all that we ever have, not yesterday, and we certainly don't have tomorrow. I do have today and I can make a difference today, so this is where I'm going to put my focus.

The pains of regret and sorrow for our mistakes are very real and there is no way of escaping their sting. Perhaps the one redeeming factor we can take away from these negative experiences, is the wisdom and the knowledge that we have gained from having gone through the experience.

Sometimes listening to elderly people who, undoubtedly, have gone through a variety of difficulties in their lives, can offer us the wisdom of the years. We can learn and find strength from the lessons they learned and the wisdom they have gained from having made it through a season of trials.

In this, we can encourage ourselves, knowing that as we successfully navigate these seasons, perhaps we too will have gained wisdom, which is a virtue most valuable and is only truly acquired through life experience.

Unfortunately, sometimes other people will stand and point the finger at us, in judgment and criticism, continuing to remind us of our failures. There is nothing we can do about what other people do or say about us. The best thing we can do about negativity from other people is to use it as an opportunity for personal growth and decide within yourself that you are not going to give other people that much power over you.

Then again, sometimes this is the best medicine for developing personal strength, through opposition. Use it as an exercise in character building, remembering that good men and women are grown, while great men and women are forged in the fire of life's struggles and trials, like the steel, that has been forged and tempered in the furnace.

I adopt the phrase, "What other people think of me is none of my business." I decide not to make it my business.

Sometimes we may think that people are thinking a certain way about us when in truth they may not be thinking of us at all and our own imagination and a sense of condemnation is the cause of our suffering. The bottom line is that *our thoughts* determine our state of happiness or misery, and we have the power to change our thoughts from negative to positive at any time, regardless of our circumstances.

If we find that we are the type of person easily offended by the slightest social slights, then perhaps we may do well to develop a "thicker skin", as to not bruise so easily. One tool for overcoming this is to regularly use personal affirmations of truths about yourself to build yourself up. As long as *you're* okay with yourself, then that's all that really matters.

In life, offenses will come. There's no getting around that. The key is overcoming obstacles effectively and learning to grow through them. All of us face challenges and need to have methods in place to re-center ourselves.

One tool that I have used for re-centering is to write out and read over a list of personal affirmations, or truths about myself. This is a list of positive things that I know to be true about myself.

Another technique is to use statements beginning with the words, "I am…" I like to use inanimate objects, for this exercise. For instance,

"*I am a light…*" I then follow this with my own thoughts about what it means to be a light. Some ideas might be,

> "*I am a light. I am able to clearly see the path before me, I am a light, a guide to those around me, I receive insights of inspiration which help me and allows me to help others, I look on the bright side and I see a bright future before me…*"

This can be a fun and an effective way to build ourselves up and to re-center.

Inna Segal, in her book, The Secret Language of Your Body, lays out an exercise which is beneficial in learning to see ourselves through the eyes of love. Here is a quote from her book:

> *"Stand in front of a mirror. Close your eyes and imagine that you are standing next to someone who loves you. If you could borrow their eyes, how would you see yourself? When you feel positive, open your eyes and look at yourself from the perspective of love."*

This exercise is transformative and can be useful in overcoming negative feelings. She continues…

> *"How do you see yourself differently? What does a person who loves you see? Affirm that you are lovable."*

Each new day is a new opportunity to be our best and to rewrite the pages of our life's story. Let's let ourselves off the hook and focus on being our best; acknowledging our weaknesses, working on them while looking ahead, forgetting our failures and shortcomings, striving to do our part to love ourselves and our fellow man.

In the game of life no one bats a thousand, but each and every day is a new opportunity to make a real difference. This kind of an attitude can change the course of our lives and cause us to live victoriously.

Live life just one day at a time, making today our only focus. In time we can learn to make our hardships and difficulties into steppingstones to maturity, wisdom and personal growth.

12

Let the Games Begin!

Several years ago, I was watching the Olympics on television and observed the procession of athletes from many nations around the world represented, with their flags waving as they paraded around for the opening ceremonies. What an amazing site; the display of colors, the spirit of joy and triumph on every face!!

They were all bursting with pride that they were so honored as to be selected to represent their respective nations in this most prestigious, international competition. What an honor! What a privilege!

It was then that I felt a deep sense of pride and achievement. I felt myself, a part of this large group of world class athletes. I realized that in celebrating them, I was celebrating the brotherhood of mankind. Together we were celebrating the human achievement; that spark of greatness which lives in every human heart. I felt such pride to be included, a member of this amazing human race.

I felt that their triumphs, were my triumphs, their joys, my joys, their pains, my pains. For that transcendent moment we, collectively were one people, with one cause, with one purpose.

Together, from all over the world, we watched, celebrating our greatness as a people; from huts, homes, villages, hamlets, in every city, metropolis; from every continent; we watched from all over the world, we were all celebrating our one amazing family!

Through watching this amazing display of human achievement, I understood the potential of the human spirit and I realized the power of having a purpose. I realized that I too have unlimited possibilities, simply because I am as one of them, a fellow human being.

In that moment I thought of the word, Ubuntu, a South African word; a celebration of humanity which translates, *"I am, because we are."* Yes, we are powerful, and triumphant; one family of man!!

13

Purpose

To have purpose is to bring meaning to life. Purpose is to life what the fragrance is to the flower. A flower with no fragrance is certainly not considered to be the most beautiful of flowers. So just what is a life lived with purpose? I'm glad you asked…

First of all, when we speak of a life of purpose, we speak of a life that is not solely focused on ourselves, but rather, is focused on helping and impacting others.

My definition of purpose speaks of a deep conviction; a driving force which is propelled by both passion and a sense of duty to serve humanity in some way. An individual who is driven by purpose is duty-bound and is fully given to fulfilling oneself through helping others. To truly live we must get a vision bigger than ourselves.

It is important that our purposes are for the good. Some people are passionate and purpose-driven for destructive things and causes. This is not the kind of purpose that I am referring to. A proper purpose-driven life is one that hurts no one along the way, while making the way for others to follow, leading by a positive example.

The beauty of living a life of purpose is that we are granted renewed energy on a regular basis. It is as though the universe assists the one operating in their purpose.

I have recalled times when I was so absorbed in my work, that the hours passed and I never stopped to eat, or felt tired, because I was purpose driven. There is no greater "high" than operating in our purpose.

The person who is purpose-driven is a much happier person than the one that is not. There is something about pouring out into others which causes us to be filled.

The highly successful TV host and philanthropist, Oprah Winfrey has a beautiful quote on helping others. Her words are:

"Helping others is the way we help ourselves."

And in the words of the great Indian leader, Mahatma Gandhi,

"The best way to find yourself is to lose yourself in the service of others."

Each individual is unique and has beauty to contribute to this world. Because of our uniqueness we have a special gift that we alone can add to the beauty of life's design. We are the only ones who can truly sing our song. We should make it our focus to discover the jewels within ourselves, develop them and bring them to life, fulfilling our unique purpose.

To the one striving to reach a desired goal and has not yet attained, become passionate right where you are. Make passion, service, empathy and purpose staples of your life, wherever you may be at the present. These qualities often bring promotion and assist us in becoming an outstanding individual, an individual of purpose. In time, we can bring these same qualities to our desired goals.

Perhaps you may be uncertain of your unique purpose. One way to find answers is to look inside ourselves. Many of the answers we seek are buried within us, like buried treasure. The way to access these secrets is to ask ourselves questions. The more that we ask ourselves questions the more answers we'll find coming to us.

I have discovered many answers this way. It is also important to take time to be quiet and still so that we can hear the answers when we are presented with them. These realizations will often come to us in a variety of ways, when we least expect them and when we are not looking for them. Simply ask the question and let the solution come to you.

Another way to discover answers from within ourselves is through writing. Writing is a proven way to discover things which may not be known to our conscious minds.

My wife Jan enjoys writing poetry. If she has a question about a situation, she will ask herself the question and then proceed to write a poem. Remarkably, the answers she has been seeking flow to her in rhyme, through her poetry.

There is no greater satisfaction in life than operating in our purpose. A fulfilled life is a life lived on purpose.

The beauty of life is that all things are interconnected and are designed to serve in cross-purposes. Operating in our purpose is one sure way to build up others, while fulfilling ourselves at the same time.

14

Thought Stream

Our thoughts are the basis of our entire lives, for each thought is a seed, bearing fruit after its own kind. I think it's important that we watch our thoughts, for they form a stream which can lead us anywhere based on our habitual thought life.

Perhaps it's not any one thought which has the potential to make or break us, but a successive train of thoughts form a guide, or a pathway to virtually any state of mind.

Sometimes people do things that are way beyond what they believed to be within their character and then they wonder, "How did I get to that point? How could I do something like this?" It may very well be the result of the direction of their thoughts.

We need to ask ourselves, "Are my thoughts good, happy thoughts or are they sad, downcast or angry thoughts?" One thought leads to another, which leads to another, and another, and so on. This is how our mind works, and we can position our thoughts to work for us or against us.

Fear can be a major factor in our choices. It is important to analyze our thoughts. We should not allow our emotions to direct our actions, but harness our thoughts and have them serve us, and not the other way around.

Each day we come to a fork in the road and face a choice. We need to ask ourselves, "What kind of thoughts am I entertaining?" or put another way, "Do my thoughts make me feel good, happy and empowered, or not?" Remember, you have the power over your thoughts.

It is important to realize that we may have one set of conscience thoughts and yet another set of unconscious thoughts. One day while sitting still I became aware of this underlaying thought stream which flows like a river beneath the surface of consciousness. This is the same thought stream active while dreaming, when we are asleep. This subconscious thought stream is operating in the background at all times, during sleep and in our waking hours.

I discovered that some of these subconscious thoughts were negative. For instance, if I were waiting on some good news and the person took longer than I expected before getting back to me, I would immediately start thinking the worse, and that perhaps things were not going to work out after all. This was being both negative and presumptuous. Many times, things did actually work out well and my negative thinking had been wasted energy.

Recognizing the power of thoughts and the importance of a healthy thought life, I began a personal program of meditation (focusing on my breath as a tool to calm my mind) and speaking positive affirmations to begin to revamp my thinking.

The next step was catching these thoughts as they arose and to stop the stream from running, replacing these thoughts with positive ones. It is said that we cannot *stop* our minds from thinking thoughts, but we do have the power to *replace* negative thoughts with positive ones.

Most importantly, even if we think a negative thought, don't voice it. Refuse to give power to it through speech. Speak only those things that you desire to come to pass. Speak life!

To change the course of our lives, we can start by changing our thoughts and our words. There is a saying, our lives follow our thoughts. That being the case, I think that we should make maintaining a healthy thought life our highest priority; thereby experiencing the fruit from these healthy thought seeds.

Here are a few quotes about the importance of correct thinking:

"If you can change your mind, you can change your life." - William James, Father of American Philosophy

"The happiness of your life depends upon the quality of your thoughts." - Marcus Aurelius, Roman Emperor

"I know for sure that what we dwell on is who we become." - Oprah Winfrey, Television Personality

If we find that our thoughts are negative and downcast, one way to switch the direction of our thoughts is to focus on everything that is going *right* and to express your gratitude. Some things we can be grateful for: being alive; being in our right mind; food to eat; eyesight; our hearing; we can walk/talk, having friends; family; our job; good health; education; flowers; birds; trees; clothes; water; transportation and a long list of things that we sometimes take for granted. There are a *million* things for which we can be grateful.

The more that we acknowledge and express our gratitude, the more our thoughts will focus on the positive things and not on the negative. This is a quick way of shifting our thinking.

If we practice verbally expressing our gratitude for everything that's going right and make this a daily practice, naming the things that went well today, this week, this month, we will develop a positive attitude which will shift our very lives to the positive, when we make this practice a habit.

It is a good exercise to make a list of the wonderful things in our lives and to read our list daily. We can upgrade this list regularly and develop an attitude of gratitude.

Learn to live life in the present moment; not yesterday, five minutes ago, or five minutes hence, focus on living and being in *this* moment. We can silence the negative chatter in our minds through turning our attention to the world around us, living in the moment, mindfully.

Yes, we have within ourselves the power to direct our thoughts. Good thoughts lead to other good thoughts and before we know it, we are carried in the direction of this positive thought stream. Our thoughts are the bricks, the building blocks of our entire world.

15

Forgiveness

Learning to forgive others is one of the most important practices to have in life. Unforgiveness is detrimental to the individual harboring the negative emotions and can undermine our best efforts. The unforgiving person actually robs him or herself of vital energy, adds wear and tear to their bodies and takes from one's own feelings of happiness.

There is even scientific evidence that the harboring of negative emotions can even be a contributing factor in illness and disease. Regardless of the offense which may have been done to us, the individual refusing to release feelings of bitterness is actually the one bringing suffering to their own life through the stressful, negative effects of negative emotions, as a result of unforgiveness.

Each of us is given so much time in our lives and none of us can afford to squander time, yet so many of us do. Some people waste years holding grudges against friends and family members, and this waste of time and energy could have been better used positively and constructively. So then, forgiveness is not a gift that we give to another person, but rather a gift that we give to ourselves.

One of the keys to learning to forgive others is to understand that every person is broken in one form or another and we've all done things that we have regretted doing, that we ourselves would like to be forgiven for. We must learn to give away those things which we desire to receive.

Forgiveness is like doing Spring Cleaning on ourselves and on our lives. Think of it as clearing away the clutter. A clean heart invites room for more love and happiness.

I understand that in some cases the offenses done to us may be great and our bitterness and anger justifiable, nevertheless the one who cannot forgive will be the one suffering from the effects of the offenses. Forgiveness is the beginning place of our healing and restoration.

If we cannot bring ourselves to being able to totally forgive someone, then at least take steps to begin the process. Write a letter of the things that you would like to say to the person. Put everything you feel into the letter and then shred or burn the letter.

In doing this exercise it is not so important that the other person hears what you have to say. In fact, it may be advisable not to share this letter with the recipient, as it may be dangerous to share it, or sharing it may be counter-productive, but it is important that we do our own work to begin to purge *our* hearts of these deep-seated feelings.

If our grief and anger are too deeply embedded it might be advisable to seek professional guidance from a counselor to navigate through these negative emotions. It is a proven fact that deep-seated, long-held negativity can lead to emotional and physical instabilities and complications.

My mother was a person who practiced forgiveness. She had far more than her fair share of griefs and great suffering throughout her life, yet she very rarely spoke of these things and carried herself in such a way that those who didn't know her story would never suspect that she had gone through anything traumatic. She always carried a calm, quiet and a caring, loving spirit.

Once someone commented to her on her great strength. My mother replied "Oh no, I'm not strong. I've just learned to give my troubles over to God."

Once, when I had been holding a grudge against someone. I had been mistreated by this individual for many years and my bitterness grew deeper with time. It finally reached a point that I could not contain it any longer.

My mother heard me mumbling to myself in anger against this person who had hurt me deeply. I was not aware that I was mumbling to myself. My mother came up to me and gently said, "Son, don't stand in your own light. Let it go."

I had never even discussed with my mother the things I was carrying, but it was clear that regardless of the circumstances, now *I* was the one who was suffering from the effects. I understood what she meant and decided to heed her wise counsel. I had to just let it go.

Nelson Mandela, Former President of South Africa is a good example of one who learned the power and the importance of forgiveness. Mandela was imprisoned wrongfully for 27 years for speaking out against the unjust and oppressive Apartheid system of racial segregation in South Africa. It is recorded that after his release from prison he continued to harbor intense feelings of anger, resentment and unforgiveness for having been wrongfully imprisoned for nearly three decades.

His intense anger was understandable and was very difficult for him to overcome. After having an epiphany on the importance of forgiving his enemies and oppressors, he decided to drop his resentments, forget the past and to move forward in love and in forgiveness.

Nelson Mandela eventually became President of South Africa and even won the Noble Peace Prize, becoming a spokesman and an ambassador advocating forgiveness and brotherly love. His life and his example have become a symbol to the power of forgiveness.

Mandela wrote that he heard this admonition from the Lord:

> *"Nelson, while you were in prison you were free, now that you are free, don't become their prisoner."*

Mandela thus decided not to remain trapped in the past. He had to let the bitterness go.

He was aware, as he later stated, that

> *"Forgiveness liberates the soul. It removes fear. That is why it is such a powerful weapon."*

Here's another powerful statement by Nelson Mandela:

> *"Resentment is like drinking poison and then hoping it will kill your enemies."*

So then, the forgiveness of others is really a gift that we give to ourselves. Through our forgiving others, we set ourselves free. This is a paradoxical truth, another one of the riddles of life.

16

Child's Play

Imagination. When we think of imagination, we think of children on the playground thinking up games and living in a world of fantasy. In our society we also see the usefulness of the imagination in the arts. It is useful to the painter, the musician or the architect, but as a whole this faculty is not recognized as too important in everyday adult life. In fact, for many people it is kept in a world of child's play.

In truth imagination is the gateway to everything!! The imagination is not only the birthplace of every thought, idea or invention ever made, but it is a faculty containing endless possibilities.

Think of people like Henry Ford, Albert Einstein, Napoleon Bonaparte, Tyler Perry, Will Smith, Elon Musk, J.K. Rowling, Steve Jobs, or Oprah Winfrey who have gone far beyond the realm of the ordinary, to tap this endless wellspring. Here are some of their own words on the subject:

> *"Even the wildest dreams have to start somewhere. Allow yourself the time and space to let your mind wander and your imagination fly."*
> *- Oprah Winfrey*

> *"Imagination rules the world." - Napoleon Bonaparte*

"My imagination is my gift, and when it merges with my work ethic, I can make money rain from the heavens." - Will Smith. This might be trash talk if it wasn't backed up by $20 million leading-man paydays.

"Imagination is more important than knowledge. Knowledge is limited. Imagination encircles the world." - Albert Einstein

"Imagination is everything. It is the preview of life's coming attractions." - Albert Einstein

Albert Einstein used his imagination to unlock secrets of the universe, never before recognized nor understood. He discovered these truths through the use of his imagination and came up with their corresponding mathematical formulas afterwards. Imagination, as with any other faculty can be strengthened with practice.

The megastar actor, Jim Carrey shared his amazing story of how he used his imagination to become a blockbuster movie actor. In an interview with Barbara Walters and in a separate interview with Oprah Winfrey, Carrey shared that while he was out of work and struggling financially, that he wrote a check to himself for 10 million dollars and dated it for three years out. He stated that during that time he *visualized* and *affirmed* that he *was already* the person he aspired to become, a famous movie star.

When Carrey began his daily program of visualization and affirmation, he was not anywhere near the person he affirmed in his words and imagined himself to be. In addition to this, he would periodically take out the "check" that he had written to himself, look at it and dream of his amazing future, as though he already had it.

Amazingly, he accomplished his goal within the timeframe that he had predetermined, using the power of his imagination!

In the book, The Power of Positive Imaging by Norman Vincent Peale, the author gives accounts of individuals who were cured of chronic health conditions through the use of their imaginations, through visualization.

Visualization is a powerful tool which sends a message to the universe; it is the way that we "put in our order" for the things which we desire to receive. The keys to being effective in this practice are "seeing" with the mind's eye, and most importantly, *feeling* enthusiasm for the wish fulfilled. It is essential to remain consistent in this practice, until the desire is fully manifested, while maintaining an attitude of belief and expectancy.

Don't be discouraged if you seem to have difficulty with visualizing clear images. Visualization works even if the images are not clear. Seeing clear images is not as important as focusing the direction of your attention, stating your intention and feeling the satisfaction of fulfillment, in advance. Focused attention is still effective and is enough to begin the attraction, even if the images are blurred or hazy.

Recently, I had a personal experience, on a much smaller scale, but nonetheless significant, using my imagination and affirmation. I wanted to attend the Houston Rodeo for my birthday, but the tickets were sold out for the opening date. That afternoon I said a short prayer, stating my request and then declared, "I *choose* to attend the rodeo. Thank you."

That same evening, to my surprise, a friend contacted us, that they had 3 rodeo tickets available, if we wanted them, as they would not be able to attend. Now we had our tickets and the very next day my wife and I went to the Houston rodeo and enjoyed the rodeo and the concert, with Country Music stars, Blake Shelton, with a special guest appearance by his wife, Gwen Stafani.

I would like to mention that when applying these principles, you must be *specific* about what it is you want. This step is not negotiable, this is the first step in the process. How can you get anywhere if you don't first decide where it is you want to go? You must set your intention.

Next, you must not be concerned about the "hows" of the equation. "How is it going to happen?" "I can't afford it." "I don't have this." "I don't have that." All of these things will become obstacles and can block the manifestation of the things we are after. On many occasions the desired requests are granted without any money involved, as when we attended the rodeo.

Here is a beautiful quote by the famous Indian leader, Mahatma Gandhi:

> *"Every moment of your life is infinitely creative, and the universe is endlessly bountiful. Just put forth a clear enough request, and everything your heart truly desires must come to you." - Mahatma Gandhi*

It is important that when using this method understand that you are not "reaching" to obtain anything. Worry, stress and "reaching" for something is counterproductive. To stress and strain in "reaching" for something simply confirms the fact that you *don't* have it, which actually blocks you from receiving it. The key is to feel the ease and the joy of *already* possessing the things you're visualizing. You have to trick your mind into accepting that you are already there!

Understanding this, we can begin to recognize this power and to use this faculty as a tool for success. So, take the time to use your imagination to explore its limitless possibilities and in the words of Oprah Winfrey,

"…let your mind wander and your imagination fly."

… to imagine becoming all that you can be. The birthplace of everything is the imagination.

17

Strategy

President Abraham Lincoln is quoted as saying,

"Give me six hours to chop down a tree and I will spend the first four sharpening the ax."

In any endeavor it is important to have a strategy, a plan of action. It is important to lay out the steps leading to our goals. Yet so many people live their lives simply going from one experience to the next without following any sort of a plan. There is a common phrase, "If you fail to plan, you plan to fail."

Strategy involves not just accomplishing the items on a checklist, but rather first giving thought to the checklist and the "whys and hows" of our list before taking any steps. Strategy requires wisdom and forethought to be effective.

Begin with a list of the things you would like to accomplish. The act of writing things down takes our ideas from the world of thought and brings them into the material world where we can more easily see the full picture and can better devise a plan for accomplishment.

Also, it is important to regularly have quiet time in our lives for reflection. I make quiet time a daily practice. This is an important step for direction and in finding the right paths. Answers can come to us when we allow this time to be still and to listen.

It's also a good idea to seek advice from experts. Consultation has provided countless answers for many individuals. The internet is a good tool to use as it is a vast resource of information on any subject. When using the internet, it is a good idea to cross reference the information to confirm its validity. Not all information on the internet is credible. Check the source's credentials and cross references.

People sometimes fail to make a plan simply because they don't know where to begin. This is where taking time to be still and seeking guidance can prove fruitful. Ask yourself questions like, "What do I want?" "Where do I see myself in five years?" "What would my ideal life look like?" These kinds of probing questions bring forth answers from within ourselves.

Writing out questions and answering them, provides a basis for moving in the right direction. Through writing things down we can easily go back over our list and remind ourselves of our steps, while creating a solid direction for moving forward. It's important to feel good about your choices before moving ahead.

Another common obstacle to growth and progress is procrastination. Ideally it would be helpful to have a motivator, a coach or a cheerleader to prod us along on our journey, but obviously this is not always available nor is it practical. One suggestion for overcoming procrastination or lack of motivation, is to find a good book that motivates you and to stay on course as you progress along. Successful people have mentors, coaches to assist them on their path. There are plenty of books that can serve this purpose.

Another way to overcome procrastination is to begin with only one item on your list of goals. Perhaps we cannot finish even one item on our list. In that case, just accomplish a portion of that which you wish to complete. Biting off too much at once can be daunting and may cause us to become discouraged.

Prioritize the items on your list. Determine which things need to come first, second, third, etc. Once this is established, go ahead and begin to complete only the first item. With this method, you will be surprised to see how much you can accomplish in a short amount of time with the greatest efficiency.

The French chemist, Louis Pasteur made the statement,

"Chance favors the prepared mind."

This statement highlights the fact that the more prepared we are, the clearer it becomes that success is accomplished less by chance and more from our adherence to the laws of success.

One important step to success is taking the right corresponding action. I like to think of this as the effect of ripples on the water. When we move in the direction of our desired goals, there are unseen forces that seem to come to our aid. To have a plan and desire is not enough. Things will begin to fall into place as we begin putting action with our words and intentions.

Our action-steps towards our goals produce energy, which causes vibrations, attracting forces to aid us. Like the ripples on the water our actions trigger corresponding reactions in the universe.

Several years ago, a friend of mine experienced this. She is a nurse and a singer who wanted to make a CD recording of her music. She told me that she didn't have the money for it, but began working on it, not being concerned about the money, or just how this was to come about.

She told me how she wrote the songs, rehearsed them, wrote out the music, preparing herself in every way. After having gone as far as she could go on her own, to her surprise a coworker unexpectedly stepped up and gave her the money to record her CD.

Sometimes if things aren't moving for us, and we find ourselves waiting for something to happen, a better plan might be to just focus on doing what we can, where we are and let the rest take care of itself. Like the line from the movie, Field of Dreams,

"If you build it, they will come."

This is putting in the work and believing and trusting in the outcome.

Many motivational speakers and life coaches teach and live by a principle, to *work harder on yourself than you do on your job.* You will certainly move forward more quickly following this advice. The more excellent *you* become, the more *valuable* you are.

There is a saying, "Fake it till you make it." Begin to get into the *feeling* of success, of already being the person you are striving to become.

Abraham Lincoln stated,

"I will prepare and someday my chance will come."

If you have not yet attained your goal, then use your present opportunity to prepare for success. Look at your wardrobe. Make sure it reflects the image you want to portray. Be well groomed. You only have one opportunity to make a good first impression.

Treat every person with respect, as you would like to be treated. The things that you know to be right, do them to the best of your ability.

Do the work, know your craft. In our competitive society, talent alone may not be enough. Prepare yourself mentally, physically, emotionally. The more prepared we are, the greater our chances of success, with the least amount of stress.

Consider this, when we were in junior high, high school and college, we carried a backpack with lots of books around with us from course to course. Some courses required several textbooks for one class.

We went through many years of preparation; courses, examinations, reports and a long list of items which all prepared us for our chosen field. It is advisable to develop a program for our personal success the same way.

Just occasionally reading a book on success and motivation is not enough. We need to be as a student, working a program for our success. Daily consistency is what transforms us into the person we aspire to become.

Our program should involve daily reading of various books related to our area of interest and on personal development. Just as the college student has many different books on a wide range of subjects, so should we do likewise.

Keep a journal and develop a curriculum for your personal development the same as one would develop one for a course. Decide what areas you want to develop, select your reading materials, writing exercises and implement your success program.

You may not necessarily need a lot of books, as some books may contain many different ideas and may constitute a large portion of the reading. The point is to carefully detail a plan and then to consistently work that plan.

Staying up on current events and working on our communication skills are also necessary steps towards working on ourselves. This is preparation for making a good first impression and helping us to be well prepared when we are presented with an opportunity.

It is also a good idea to keep a checklist of things necessary for our success, preparing for a good encounter, ahead of time.

Afterwards, review how we came across in our encounter. List the things that we did right and those things that we didn't do so well, so that we can work on polishing ourselves, becoming our very best. Just the recognition of our areas of weakness provides us feedback, giving us awareness, which is one step towards overcoming in these areas of deficiency.

Of course, your program needs to include time to study your craft and devoting time to its development. And again, a good program is one that makes personal development our highest priority.

Be specific in developing your plan. Put it all on paper. If you need finances, how much do you need? Write it down in your journal. If you need a certain contact, write that down. Opportunity presents itself to us as we progress toward our goals.

Writing down the specifics of your strategy is a vital step to its fulfillment. You don't have to know how you will accomplish everything on your list, but write it down anyway.

The most important companion to accompany us on our journey to success is daily consistency. Through the habitual, daily practice of disciplines, we develop skill, character, stamina and patience, all vital tools of our success.

No one would think of building a house or establishing a business without a strategy. The same is true in life. Make a plan and then work your plan carefully, steadily and consistently. This is the pathway to being our best and a path to greater success.

18

When the Bottom Falls Out

What do we do when the bottom falls out? Where can we find strength when we are at our wits' end? I've heard it said that this life journey is more like a marathon, than a sprint. It is for certain that in a marathon you can't sprint all the way. In life we will have hills and valleys and times when we have to simply stop and cannot continue.

A life crisis may be a divorce, the death of a loved one, losing our job, losing our home, a sickness and so many other unexpected life events. It is important to know how to properly navigate the many varied conditions of life.

In life, we all go through our share of difficulties. Some people grow stronger through it, while others are devastated by the storm. So, we ask the question again, "What do we do when the bottom falls out?"

Keeping our emotional equilibrium at these times is crucial. Pure emotion is never a good guide for navigating life's hurdles and this is especially the case at difficult times.

The news headlines are filled with cases of individuals who did not handle their problems well and in some cases have created even more problems for themselves and for others. A good principle to live by is to always keep a level head. Stress and anxiety only add to an already difficult situation, complicating matters further.

Understand that effective navigation of any kind requires the proper tools. Many people turn to spirituality as a means of finding strength and guidance in difficult situations.

The best place to start when facing a crisis is to stop, allow yourself to become still. Some people try to continue life as if nothing has changed, becoming absorbed in work or something to distract themselves from the reality of the situation. This is not a good tactic for eventually we will have to confront our deep-seated emotions head on. Burying our emotions can lead to bigger problems down the road.

I think that it is always a good idea to cultivate a hopeful attitude towards life in general and especially at these times of adversity. Even though we may have suffered a great loss, keep the hope of coming through this season of life and realize that it is just a season. Even in the natural, we encounter many different seasons and storms are followed by periods of beauty and new growth. Believe in the hope of a better tomorrow. There is an old song which states, "This too shall pass."

We human beings are powerful, competent, creative and highly intelligent beings. We possess more power than we may realize. While this is true, it's also important to recognize that we are also fragile and sometimes we need additional assistance. Some burdens are simply too heavy for us to bear on our own. It is wise to know our own limits and know when it is time to seek assistance.

It is good to have the support of friends and loved ones and to welcome their help. Sometimes we need to be carried in life. As in the lyrics to this Bill Withers' classic, "We all need somebody to lean on."

Sometimes in a difficult season, we will feel a need to pull away and to be alone. That is to be expected. But it is advisable not to be alone for too long, as this can lead to depression and a sense of hopelessness. Having strong support from friends and loved ones can make all of the difference.

If you feel that you need help making it through a difficulty, ask for help from a friend or someone you trust to help you carry the burden. Having someone to talk to can be enormously beneficial. Know that there are people who will suffer with us, who will assist us with carrying our burdens.

For those of us who witness someone that is struggling with a hardship, understand that this is an opportunity for you to make a difference. Be proactive, go to them and offer a kind word or offer your assistance.

Many times people have difficulty asking for help under the best of circumstances, and they probably are not likely to ask for it at these times either. Be the help that they need, the shoulder to lean on, the arms to uphold them. Step up to the plate and make a difference.

During these times of distress, it is important to know where to find help. Here are some avenues to explore during these difficult times; find strength through reading a good book, talking with a professional counselor, listening to music or to inspirational teachings, going to church or finding a support group are all useful tools for navigating through difficult situations. I have found these tools to be helpful and to be a good source of strength and guidance.

Finally give it time. Time has a way of healing many hurts and situations. Time can sometimes give us clarity when we allow space for the smoke to clear away.

Personally, I have found strength in my faith. In drawing upon this inexhaustible resource, I find that I can not only better navigate through the difficulties of life, but I can come out on the other side, stronger, peaceful and centered, able to carry on and move ahead in my life.

Know that you too can overcome. The human spirit is powerful and more resilient than we sometimes recognize. Nature provides us with a beautiful symbol for overcoming, in the lotus flower.

The lotus flower, the national flower of India, can survive in both fresh, shallow waters and muddy swamps and can re-germinate for thousands of years. This remarkable flower symbolizes survival, overcoming adversity, rebirth, and purity of heart, mind, and spirit under any circumstances.

The beautiful, elegant, pink blossoms and broad petals exemplify its grace and resilience. Many cultures use the lotus as the symbol of longevity, honor, good fortune, and victory.

Human beings have successfully come through every difficulty known to man and you are no different. You too can overcome. You have untapped resources within you and like the lotus, you are more resilient and more beautiful than you know.

19

Relay Race

In life we can get more of practically everything. We can get more money, we can acquire more friends, we can obtain more property, more success.

We can get more of practically everything in life, except time. Time is the one thing that we have that is irreplaceable.

Time is one of our most valuable gifts. It is a gift because it is indeed precious and should be valued as a treasured gift.

Our lives are a treasured asset and the most important thing that we possess. Therefore, our time is vital and just how we choose to spend it and with whom, should be at the very top of our list of priorities.

Here is a quote from the success coach, Jim Rohn,

"Days are expensive. When you spend a day, you have one less day to spend. So make sure you spend each one wisely."

Many people don't fully appreciate the value of their time, until having experienced a hardship or loss which makes us reevaluate our lives and our priorities.

When I lost my mother several years ago, I began to reflect over my life and my purpose. I thought of a relay race and imagined that those who have gone on before us in this race have now passed the baton onto us and now is our opportunity to "run our lap" in this great life race.

Others have finished their lap and have passed the baton onto us. Now that we are in the race, what are we doing with this opportunity?

Some people squander time, and instead of running their race are spending time, sometimes years, living mediocre lives. Others are so busy in someone else's race that they are unaware of their own.

Some people squander their time away over regrets, hates, malice, and unforgiveness, wasting years of their lives on things which really are not so important in the final assessment. And all for what? My advice, pick up your baton and get back in the race!

Running your race is fulfilling your purpose in life. If you don't know what that purpose is, then find a purpose, a cause, get busy working on it and make your life count by focusing on something bigger than yourself.

Realize the truth that today, right now is your opportunity to "run your lap" and see each day as a treasure and a new opportunity, to right the wrongs of the past and to make your life count for the better, not just for ourselves, but to help others as we run our race together.

A relay race is not run alone, but the very nature of the race is built upon the strengths of the combined runners. This translates in life as supporting those who are connected to us, as we never know what part people may be playing or perhaps will play in our life story, or the vital part that we may be playing in someone else's life.

Finally, let us remember to keep our eyes on running our race and on finishing it as we have purposed. It is a wonderful thing to have the opportunity to be in this race. How we finish it is up to us.

20

Victor or Victim?

People generally have a view of life that is either positive or negative. Obviously, we all have ups and downs in life and experience a wide range of emotions. But what is our habitual tendency? Here is a question we need a ask ourselves, "Am I a victor or a victim?"

VICTOR TRAITS

Positive
Proactive
Forward thinking
Forgetting the mistakes of the past
Seeker of truth
Focused on strengths
Boundless thoughts of possibilities
Focused on self-improvement, and on building up and helping others
Character development as a top priority
Focused on values
Disciplined
Self sufficient
Appreciates self
Progressive
Focused on goals
Full of faith
Self-Love

VICTIM TRAITS

Negative
Focused on the past
Reactive
Limiting thought life
Focused on self (selfish, self-conscious, self-pity)
Filled with regrets/guilt
Focused on weaknesses
Blaming others
Fear driven
Filled with doubts
Anticipates failure
Critical of self and others
Self-Rejection
Lack of initiative
Dependent
Undisciplined
Stagnant

Always feeling left out, "Why not me? When is my chance?" These negative thoughts attract more rejection. With this kind of thinking we are literally sending out rejection signals, which are met with more rejection.

We cannot be a victor and a victim at the same time, because one cancels out the other. Every time we embrace the victim mentality, we undermine our progress forward.

It is true that at times we all may display characteristics of both the victor and the victim. For example, individuals who have achieved great heights in life most likely have gone through a period of "victimhood" on their way to success. It is also entirely possible to have certain areas of our lives which tend one way or the other and in certain areas of our lives, we may have tendencies of both.

The downward spiral happens when we *dwell* in the victim state of mind. This destructive mindset actually repels positivity and rejects the victor mindset and may even reject individuals that are positive.

I confess that I have gone through seasons of my life where I had adopted the victim mindset and had to learn, firsthand of its destructive nature.

When I lost my first wife to cancer in 2005, my life took a nosedive, and I was in a prolonged state of grief, shock and bewilderment. My entire life was thrown off course.

The repercussions from this loss were drastic and lasted for many years. I was unaware that I had gradually shifted into thinking and acting like a victim. Every area of my life reflected this downcast mindset and I didn't know how to pull myself out of this slump. It took me several years to even begin to regain my footing and to begin rebuilding my life.

My turnaround began when I recognized that I was living in a victim state of mind and recognized that I was standing in my own way. I began to work on overcoming this state of living, beginning with addressing my words and my thoughts.

As long as I continued searching for answers outside myself, I never found them. It wasn't until I stopped searching "out there" and started looking "in here", that I began to find the answers to rebuilding my life.

I cannot say that I have "arrived" in my life, as we all know that in life we never "arrive", as this life is not about the destination, but about the journey. I can say that as I work on overcoming my past and embrace new possibilities for my future, that today I am experiencing more of the benefits of living in the *victor* state and am enjoying greater happiness and fulfillment.

I now strive to maintain a victor mindset, through a daily process of thought reconditioning, replacing negative thoughts with positive ones.

No one decides to adopt a victim mindset, it develops through our life experiences and through the ways that we cope. For example, sometimes people that have experienced trauma in their lives build "walls" around themselves to guard against possible assaults in the future.

These "walls" are boundaries we set up to keep people away. This may serve as "protection" in some cases, however in many cases, these walls imprison us, causing us to approach life with trepidation, preventing us from living a full life of joy and peace.

Another characteristic of the victim mindset is the belief that the *fates* are somehow against us and are preventing our progress in life. The truth is that there are no fates opposing us. It's our own negative thoughts, fears, expectations and *beliefs that we are being opposed* which are the very things opposing us, or as this quote from William Shakespeare's dramatic history play, Julius Caesar states,

"The fault, dear Brutus, lies not within our stars, but within ourselves..."

Unknowingly many people oppose themselves, counting themselves out of the race. Whatever we believe to be true *will* be true for *us*. Whether it's actually true or not has no bearing on this. The law of attraction will *make* whatever we believe to be true, actually true for us.

The law of attraction works on the basis of, "like attracts like." Positive things attract positive things and negative things attract negative things.

Everything in the universe is under the jurisdiction of the force of attraction. This is the same force which holds the planets in place, governing their orbits, sustaining order in the universe's billions of galaxies; the same force which connects the cells of our bodies. It causes animal, plant and fish species to group together to form flocks, herds, and schools.

It brings people together and is that which causes our thoughts to attract those things on a similar frequency. Through the law of attraction negative, fearful thoughts and feelings will attract the circumstances, people and events that are on this same frequency, of negativity.

The same is true for positive thoughts and feelings. Positivity brings more positive things into our lives. Attraction is the force operating in the entire universe. It's simply the physics and the mathematics of the universe.

In order to live the victorious life, we must renew our minds daily and abandon all of the victim practices. As former President Barack Obama stated in one of his speeches,

"We must work on ourselves."

One way that we can work on ourselves is to learn to live life in the present moment. The popular, self-help teacher, Eckhart Tolle emphasizes the power of living life in the present moment. The basic premise is the idea that the past is over, and the future is but a hope, a dream. All that we ever really have is this present moment.

This moment is the only time that is. This practice is the practice of mind-fulness, that is, being in the present moment, attentively and non-judgmentally.

This is the power I have over my life. I have the control over this moment and therefore I have the control over any and every moment, when I make only *this present moment* my only focus.

Since neither the past nor the future are actually in the present moment, then why give them such power over our lives? This moment is the only moment we ever have. Learn to live life in the *now*. It is important when practicing being *present,* that we practice being non-judgmental. Simply observe the world as it is, not as we define it to be. This is a powerful tool for reducing stress.

Here is an affirmation for this day, this hour, for this moment:

> *This present moment is brand new. There never has been, nor will there ever be a moment like this. Do not color this moment with moments from the past, nor expectations of the future, for this moment is a new beginning, a new birth, filled with endless possibilities! In this moment lies new choices, new horizons and new opportunities. I make the choice to abide in and appreciate the beauty in this present moment.*

Making the choice to live our lives, one moment at a time, is one sure way to alleviate stress and anxiety, while enjoying a fuller life experience. The experience of being *present* allows us to enjoy the colors, the touch, smells, tastes, sights and sounds that are all around us all the time, only now we truly realize it and can appreciate it.

This is the difference between *looking* and *seeing.* Many times, in fact, the majority of the time we may be looking but don't really "see" because we are somewhere lost in our thoughts. Practicing being present, until it becomes a habit will yield positive results in your life.

To overcome a victim mindset, understand that there are answers to aid us in transcending these states of mind. To make the transition from the victim mindset to the victor mindset is one of the themes of this entire book.

Making this transition requires a daily, consistent program of positive speech, positive thoughts and actions and most importantly developing internal *feelings* of empowerment, confidence and self-love. I might add the importance of reading the right books (this one, of course!) which will help you to stay on track. We cannot make the shift from a negative mindset to a positive one without a consistent input of new information.

Here is an affirmation of victory:

"In order to be victorious in my life, I choose the path of the victor. I abandon thoughts of victimhood and I embrace my strengths, my uniqueness and my individuality. I am the captain of my soul; I am a victor, and I will not accept anything less."

21

Il Dolce Far Niente!

There is a beautiful Italian phrase, "Il dolce far niente", which is translated as, *"The sweetness of doing nothing."* The words, "doing nothing" imply living life *on purpose*, with a good balance of working and then enjoy taking quality time for pleasure; learning to let go and to find joy in rest and relaxation.

My wife, Jan, being English, says that many Europeans criticize Americans for our inability to slow down and actually enjoy life. It is said that we eat too fast, without really enjoying the food, that we don't sit and relax very long after meals to linger and visit; that we are impulsive, always on our cell phones and even when we're supposed to be relaxing, we are not really "all there", but rather our minds are still at the office or elsewhere, certainly not in the moment.

Admittedly, we Americans tend to live in a fast-paced society where maximum production and the bottom line have replaced taking time to slow down, rest and savor our moments of R&R.

I would agree that we need a little more of *il dolce far niente* in our world, where we are encouraged to take enough time to really enjoy the full spectrum of the joys and wonders of living; to occasionally revel in the beauty of pure idleness, without feeling guilty for doing so.

The only way to acquire *"the sweetness of doing nothing"* is to clear our calendars, drop everything and allow ourselves to revel in simply *being*, with no agenda, and enjoy its sweetness! In fact, this shouldn't be an event for just a couple of times per year, but I think it's about adopting a new way of living our lives, daily.

Certain cultures include rest in their regular schedules. In Israel the Sabbath Day is observed weekly as a day to rest and businesses are closed in the weekly observance of it. During this time everyone is encouraged to do no work, but to enjoy total rest, relaxation and recuperation.

In a number of nations around the world, the Siesta is practiced a few days a week, which is a time between 2:00 and 5:00 PM where again, many stores are closed and those who want to participate are invited to relax and enjoy this quiet time.

I think that adding regular times of rest to our lifestyle here in the US will only increase our efficiency in the long run. This practice will certainly bring more "sweetness" to our lives and give us that much more to give when we are called upon to produce. It may seem ironic, but as the saying goes, "Sometimes less is more."

22

The Chicken or the Egg?

Every successful person has a formula for that success. Or put another way, to every effect there is a cause. Success builds on success.

Centering oneself, having quiet time, contemplative meditation, all of these induce, creativity, happiness and empowerment.

A positive mind produces positive results. For instance, working out in the morning leads to wanting to improve yourself in other areas of your life. I experienced this recently and made a most interesting discovery.

I began practicing mindfulness, which is simply being in the moment, for example eating a meal mindfully is to savor the tastes, textures and colors of the food. It means to slow down, look around and to make eating a meal an actual experience. In doing so, I discovered that the food tasted that much better and the experience left me feeling happy, full and satisfied. I continued being mindful throughout the day, taking a few moments to be in the moment, purposefully.

The next day I decided to start working out again after several months off. I also began practicing my music again and to attend to many of the things that I had procrastinated on doing for weeks. I started to realize a pattern here.

There is a famous old question, "What came first, the chicken or the egg?" In regard to my situation, which came first? Was it the sudden desire to better myself in various areas of my life, or was it the practice of mindfulness meditation? I began to see that the mindfulness was the cause, and my actions were the result, or the effects of that internal change.

The more that I practiced this, slowing down and being in the moment, I began to notice a shift in my thoughts and focus. I became much more at peace, inspired, happier and empowered. From this simple experience I began to realize that to change our lives in a consistent way, the change must begin within, and this change will then be reflected outward in our life experience.

As we, *ourselves* become better, our lives and our world will become better. Instead of focusing on the effects that we want, why not go to the cause?

I have discovered that so often we live so much of lives in our heads. Sometimes we are so busy thinking about the past, or worrying about the future that we don't experience the present, let alone enjoy it.

The secret of this mindfulness training is that just a few minutes of mindfulness every day goes a long way. Through this simple practice we can make every day that much brighter and more productive, with less effort.

23

Vision

Just what does it mean to have vision? Obviously, we are speaking of something more than just eyesight. Vision, as used here refers to an inner vision; the ability to see beyond what is before us, to see ahead to greater possibilities.

Every great advance in our human development began with someone having vision to see what began as only possibilities. Coupled with our vision is a faith, a belief in that which cannot be seen nor touched, but is a thought, a reaching into the unknown to bring forth into manifestation that which before was unseen.

The list of visionaries who brought their dreams to fruition is long. It consists of inventors, writers, architects, athletes, explorers, musicians, lay persons, pioneers, artists, business people, housewives and those from every facet of life.

Into every human heart has come ideas, creations, and great potential exploits. It is only the visionary however, who sees it through to the end and brings forth the idea, making it a reality.

Yes, vision is one side of the coin, the other is action. Together there are no limits to our possibilities. Vision is the spark that ignites the flame of inspiration, giving substance to our dreams, carrying them, and in due course, bringing them forth into physical manifestation. Never underestimate the power of a vision.

A vision needs to be developed. Even in the purely physical sense of the word, vision must be clear in order that the image be fully recognized in detail. So, it is with our inner vision.

Some ways to develop our inner vision is to first write it down. In writing down our thoughts and dreams we begin to bring them from our imagination into the physical world.

Colleen O'Neill, a friend I met while attending college in Seattle, wrote a book entitled, "Writing Your Future." In her book she shares her story of how she documented details of her ideal life, as she wished it to be five years down the road, her wish list, her vision. She listed specific details of the things she desired to have accomplished during those years.

Colleen told me that several years later she stumbled upon this list and discovered that every detail of what she had written on this list, had all been realized, within the time frame that she had predetermined. I have experienced similar results in my own life.

One technique is to practice actively using your imagination to see and feel yourself as having already accomplished your desired goal.

The late Frederick J. Eikerenkoetter II, better known as "Reverend Ike," used the phrase, "Get full of the feeling." He is also quoted as using his made-up term, "Full-feel-ment", emphasizing the importance of maintaining positive *feelings* regarding the things you are pursuing in your vision, as though already possessing them, which brings them forth. One must *feel* the same feelings beforehand, that one would experience *after* having experienced the wish, fulfilled.

One other thing to consider on the path to accomplishment is the practicality of failure. That's right, failure. Many people are counted out of the game because of their repeated failures. Actually, failure is a necessary component of success.

> *"Develop success from failures. Discouragement and failure are two of the surest steppingstones to success." - Dale Carnegie*

Here is an interesting quote,

> *"I've missed more than nine thousand shots in my career. I've lost almost three hundred games. Twenty-six times I've been trusted to take*

*the game-winning shot and missed. I've failed over and over and over
again in my life."*

He goes on to say...

"... and that is why I succeed."

These words were spoken by Michael Jordan, one of the undisputed, greatest basketball players of all time! Understand that sometimes our failures can
become our greatest teachers.

The above quote by Michael Jordan was posted in the Chicago Tribune
newspaper May 19, 1997, in an article entitled, "Without Failure Jordan Would
Be False Idol" by Eric Zorn. In the article Zorn further stated,

> *"Those who are afraid to fail will coast though life and never come
> close to their potential. Failure-honest failure despite genuine effort-is
> an underrated teacher and motivator as well as a sign that one is striv-
> ing at close to full capacity."*

Obviously, it was not these game statistics which earned Michael Jordan
his high ratings, and deemed him *the greatest basketball player in history,* but
they do show clear evidence of the importance of the failure component to
success, as well as drive home the fact that our record of failures may perhaps
become our greatest ally to superstardom! The only way that we can ever *truly*
fail is give up and decide not to try anymore.

Don't be discouraged by your failures, just get back up and go again. Return your focus to the goal, to the vision. A persistent focus on a vision, together with passion, a sustained enthusiasm, belief in its fulfillment, together
with action is a powerful force to surmount the greatest odds and is a proven,
time-tested formula for success.

24

Perhaps…

Albert Einstein was one of the greatest minds in history and discovered many astounding breakthroughs in the fields of science, physics and in mathematics, establishing the foundation for modern science. Here he shares some of his profound truths.

Einstein, speaking on the vastness of the universe and on the rumors that he was an atheist...

> *"I'm not an atheist. The problem involved is too vast for our limited minds. We are in the position of a little child entering a huge library filled with books in many languages. The child knows someone must have written those books."*

This statement raises a question and suggests that perhaps the universe with its infinite stars and galaxies didn't "just happen", but perhaps there is a profound intelligence which supports and maintains this grand design of life, sustaining the balance on earth and in the universe. Interesting thought...

Here is another one of Einstein's pearls of wisdom...

> *"Everything is determined, every beginning and ending, by forces over which we have no control. It is determined for the insect, as well as for the star. Human beings, vegetables, or cosmic dust, we all dance to a mysterious tune, intoned in the distance by an invisible piper."*

Perhaps. What if Einstein's statements are true that there is an "Invisible Piper" who is governing all that is? Certainly, this would explain or fill in the blanks for many of our questions of the beginnings of life, of our existence and of the uniformity of life here on the earth.

It is amazing to consider that the universe has existed for millions of years and the planets in our own solar system are so precise in their orbits that we can set our watches and gage it all right down to the millisecond, establishing our seasons, hence our reality for thousands of generations!

Consider this; while walking down the street we observe a parcel of ground, with no signs of life. A short time later we pass this same parcel and observe life, plants, growing in this same spot. Our entire planet is charged, pregnant with life-giving energy, which is in constant operation to maintain the balance of life here on earth.

Or consider that much of the food that we enjoy sprouts from the earth, (apples, oranges, grapefruit, lemons, kiwi, bananas, in fact, *all* of our fruits and vegetables) are provided by nature for our essential sustenance, with delicious flavors, appealing to our tastebuds.

Our planet earth is the perfect distance from the sun to sustain life here. If we were any closer, we would burn up, if we were any further away, we would freeze. The rains which fall, watering the earth, which has taken place since the dawn of mankind, let's us know that we are in good hands.

From this we *do* know for sure that this Life Force which sustains all life in the entire universe, is benevolent and is always working towards our well-being and towards our welfare and has done so, sustaining life on earth for countless centuries. The present deviations from this perfect balance are the result of the inventions and interventions of mankind.

Perhaps there's truth in Einstein's words, that "someone must have written these books." Who can say? Perhaps there's more to this than meets the eye... Perhaps my part in the grand scheme of life is more significant than I realize... Perhaps there's more to the story...

Perhaps...

25

Unplugged

The world today is filled with so many wonderful advances in medicine, in technology, in science and in practically every area of human development, we have advanced exponentially over the last 200 years. In fact, there are so many new advances every day that we can barely keep up.

While this is a great thing, we also need to make sure that we keep a balance. Many people today are becoming disconnected with other people, on a personal level, because of these technological advances. They are on their cell phones and other gadgets constantly and as a result are becoming detached from actual personal, physical interactions.

We've all seen it; a table full of people where everyone is on their cell phones, and no one is engaging with anyone at the table! Young people are especially susceptible to this because of society's pressures to "keep pace" with the latest fads, gadgets, trends and fashions and as a result many people are unknowingly abusing these things.

Today, I observed several individuals on their phones while walking! Some people even walk across the street in traffic, while on their phones, oblivious to the world around them. The results of this disconnection in society is having negative consequences.

One basic area which has suffered from these advances is the simple practice of letter writing. In some arenas handwriting is practically a lost art. A handwritten letter or note is much more personal than an email or a text message.

In some classrooms today students are encouraged to complete their assignments on the computer and as a result legible handwriting is becoming compromised. It would be a shame if the practice of handwriting were to become a thing of the past. Image that!

I have found myself being affected by this trend. Recently, I wrote a letter to a friend and found it almost felt foreign to hold an ink pen and to write a letter, because of my tendency these days, to write nearly all of my correspondence on the computer.

Also in computer writing, auto correct has allowed us to avoid matters of spelling and punctuation. Why not challenge ourselves; turn this function off or better yet get in the habit of occasionally writing a letter with pen and paper?

One way we can sharpen our penmanship is by keeping a journal, using pen and paper. This is a way to practice legible handwriting while journaling, which is known to be a proven path to self-discovery.

Here's something else we can practice "gadget-less." My wife, Jan, enjoys doing any needed math calculations in her head. She doesn't use a calculator. This is another way that we can give our brains a workout from time to time.

Too many hours of daily screen time are having negative repercussions in many people. Anything that's done in excess can have negative consequences.

We hear about these negative effects in the news, of depression and obesity in adults and even in children today. As a result of this weight gain and lack of exercise, diabetes is on a rise among our youth. Instead of getting the physical exercise of playing outdoors, as many of us did as kids, so many children today are now spending countless hours indoors, on their phones, video games and devices.

Parents might do well to encourage more physical exercise for their children, monitor their time online and be aware of what they're viewing. This is good advice for children as well as for adults.

Some families practice a "no phone zone", in the home, perhaps around the dinner table. Not a bad idea. So much of what we receive by way of the internet, television and on social media is mind-numbing and some is of a negative nature. Not all of it is negative, but a large percentage is, and if we don't redirect our own thinking, we may become influenced by negativity.

The things that we see, hear and read influence us on a subconscious level. It is for this reason that we should be careful what we allow to habitually fill our minds.

If we find that something we read or heard is having a negative effect upon us, then we can take steps to counter this negative progression. In order to change our feelings, it is vital to change our thoughts. To begin with, unplug, get alone and allow yourself to relax.

One effective exercise to redirect our thinking is to make a list of 10 or more happy events in our life, or times when we accomplished something great or were courageous, and to reflect back over this "feel-good list" and recapture the feelings we experienced at those times. Every time we feel a sag in our energy and positivity, we can read over our list. The same feelings we experienced at those times will return to us as we reflect upon and revisit our moments of joy and our peak performances.

The success coach, Jim Rohn made the statement,

"Give whatever you are doing and whoever you are with, the gift of your attention."

When interacting with anyone, out of respect, put your phone away. It is offensive to others, in social situations, to be continually distracted by our phones. This type of behavior is actually saying to those around us, "You're not important." This is making something or someone else more important than the individual that's right in front of us.

It's a good practice to fully engage and to be acutely focused on the individuals we're engaging with and not become distracted by other things. Additionally, replying to phone calls and text messages in a timely manner is also another practice which conveys our regard and respect for others.

One thing which has become commonplace, is to speak loudly or listen to music loudly on our cellphones while in public settings. Many people do this with an unconscious awareness of those around them. I have found this practice to be offensive to me, especially when it takes place while I am at my job, playing background piano music, while having to compete with the music from someone's cellphone. I have had this experience more times than I'd like to admit.

Our phone conversations should be in private. Certainly, I'm not interested in hearing the details of a stranger's business and I certainly don't want other people listening in on my conversations.

All of these practices are ways of forcing ourselves, our personal lives, our musical interests and our personal interests upon others. Though often unsaid, we will be resented for this blatant intrusion of privacy. Practice giving to others the respect that you would want to receive.

Now let's look at things we can do to unplug. It might be a good idea to limit the amount of time we spend on our gadgets. As was stated earlier, having a balance is important.

Take time to be outdoors and leave your cell phone and other gadgets off, or at least have times in the day away from using them and experience the beauty that's around you. Establishing this new habit may seem hard to do at first, but like with most things, this can develop over time.

Just think, 100 years ago no one had a cell phone, laptop, tablet or iPad and we survived just fine without them. In fact, mankind has existed on this planet, for thousands of years without any of these inventions, and we have thrived, so it won't hurt us to take a few moments away from them, to enjoy the simple things and thereby enhance the quality of our lives and personal relationships.

The best way to unplug is simply to unplug. Decide that you are not going to let anything external to yourself run your life.

I have had several occasions when I went on my phone to do something specific, got sidetracked, visiting a social media site, or viewing a news headline briefly, became distracted, then twenty minutes to an hour later forgot the reason I pulled out my phone in the first place. Sound familiar? This is one indication that our gadgets may be having too much power over our own choices.

One simple step I took to help with this, is to create a new page on my phone or tablet desktop and to place my social media apps on this last page of my device. I don't put any other apps on this page. This way I don't see them when I go to my email or phone book, putting them out of sight, out of mind. Then I only visit these apps when *I decide* to see them and this way I'm never caught off guard, being distracted from my intended purpose.

Since I've started doing this, I have discovered that I now have more control over the use of my time. I may be gathering more unread messages in my inbox before responding, but at least now I am in control of my time rather than being distracted by every post that shows up. Besides, so much of this information is really not so important to our lives and our purposes.

Perhaps you could schedule only specific times during the day or the week for going on social media and thereby limit its influence in your life. You will certainly have more peace of mind, richer relationships and you can use this extra time away from these devices to be *in the moment,* to accomplish other things, "gadget-less" and to appreciate more of life's beauty.

26

Unsung Heroes

So much of the news that we hear today is of a negative nature. If we were to judge the state of humanity by the 11:00 PM news broadcast, we would see a picture ever so dim. Fortunately, this is not the full picture. There is goodness in the world.

So just where might we go to witness some of this good news? Actually, it is surprisingly near. Every day there is a world of unsung heroes spreading love and goodness all around us. Perhaps you may be one of them.

On my job at Houston Methodist hospital, I see so many people in the healthcare system who are continually giving kindness and care to patients, visitors and to their coworkers. Here we can find a world of unsung heroes. Yes, as in the words of the song, believe it or not, this really is "a wonderful world!"

Many of these individuals make spreading love and goodness a way of life. There are heroes in every facet of life, and not just in health care.

When I lived in Seattle, I experienced one of these heroes, a friend from my church, a wonderful man named Wallace Chocklon. Wallace is a rare type of person; loyal, loving and consistent. I have known him for many years and he has always remained the same.

Wallace is jovial, friendly and quick to offer help in any way that he can. He has had many hardships in his life, but this has in no way diminished his love and service to humanity. He makes family, friendship and service to others his priority.

Wallace possesses a vast array of skills which he readily utilizes to help a wide network of people. He is a handyman, skilled in carpentry, plumbing, construction, auto mechanics and a plethora of other skills and abilities.

He is an outstanding athlete, having had successful football and wrestling careers himself, and though currently retired, athletics still continue to play an important role in his life. He coaches and referees many diverse sports including wrestling, softball, football, baseball and basketball. He is an excellent mentor and role model to many young, aspiring athletes.

Wallace is also a musician, playing a little piano, a singer and is involved in ministry. What makes Wallace a hero is that he gives of himself with his whole heart to others on a consistent basis. He is truly one of the most genuine and kindest people I have ever known.

Whenever anyone needs advice or assistance Wallace is there to help and he has been there for me personally, for my family and for countless others. Wallace Chocklon is a living example of the goodness that is alive in our world.

Yes, we can find heroes all around us if we look for them.

Another unsung hero is a friend of mine, Roy Griffin, of Roy's Hair Care in Missouri City, Texas. I have known Roy for a few years now and every time I see him, he has a smile and an encouraging word.

Roy told me that every day of his life he purposes to make a difference, doing something good for someone, every day. He said it doesn't have to be anything big, but he too makes encouraging and helping others a priority.

Roy has been married 54 years and has been cutting hair for about that same amount of time and says that he has met thousands of people from all walks of life. Many of the people who have taken his advice in life have greatly benefited. I am encouraged and empowered every time I am around him.

Conversely, Roy has also seen many people who have met with disaster, who failed to see the importance of taking sound advice or making the right choices in life. He speaks with emotion about the people he has dealt with and it is clear that he holds a deep care and concern for the well-being of others.

Roy, like so many other heroes, are to be commended, for they are, each and every one, making a difference in the world and in many cases are rescuing those of us who may be living on the edge. We all need a boost from time to time and it is the people like Roy and Wallace who are making a real difference in our world. They are heroes, as the moon and stars that light the night sky.

Roy has many friends of all ages, and from all walks of life. He has touched the lives of countless people and this goodness is continually returned to him from grateful hearts who have benefited from his care and concern. People who go to him for a haircut often leave with so much more than just a cut; they leave with a smile, a new lease on life and with renewed inspiration.

Roy shared a couple of his favorite sayings with me, which he has graciously allowed me to share with you. He likes to live by this motto: *"If it's to be, it's up to me."* That's a powerful statement of initiative. Yes, we all can make a difference.

Another thing Roy says:

"There are only three kinds of people in the world: those that make things happen, those who watch things happen and those that ask, 'What just happened?'"

I think that Roy, like so many others, is a living example of the benefits of living a life of purpose. There are unsung heroes everywhere, if we just keep our eyes open, we'll see them.

I would like to mention a couple of dear friends who have been heroes in my life, George and Marilyn Duff from Mercer Island, Washington. Unfortunately, George passed away recently, but I will cherish his memory and celebrate both George and Marilyn as unsung heroes.

George, who served as the former President of the Seattle Chamber of Commerce, was noted for his love and support of people and his generosity extended into my life. He was a very successful businessman who practiced principles for all to aspire to. Both he and Marilyn are examples of how we, individually, can make a real difference in life.

George Duff's life of care and compassion has been compared to the character George Bailey in the movie, It's a Wonderful Life. So many of the good deeds done by this couple are undocumented and were carried out in secret. Both George and Marilyn Duff's life and character are exemplary and must be included in my list of unsung heroes.

Here is a brief excerpt from the Seattle Times regarding George Duff. The current president and CEO of the chamber, Rachel Smith, said:

"Duff was one of the first regional leaders to expand the Seattle metro area's connections to the rest of the country and the world."

The article highlights his part in the establishment of the Seattle Mariners Baseball Team.

"Duff was involved in the negotiations to have Redmond-based Nintendo of America buy the baseball team in 1992. The previous owner had plans to move the team to Florida."

The article continues…

"After scrutiny from Major League Baseball, which opposed a non-U.S. or Canadian group buying a U.S. team, Nintendo bought the Mariners for $125 million and sold the team for $661 million to First Avenue Entertainment in 2016."

Both George and Marilyn were supporters of many people. Their hearts are in service to humanity. Here is one of George's sayings,

"You can get a lot done if you don't care who gets the credit."

To name all of the accomplishments and the significant contributions of this couple would produce a book of unwieldy size, so I'll limit my discussion to these few facts.

I will be forever grateful to them, and through their example I have become a better person. I will strive to model their goodness in my own life.

There are many people that I would like to include in my list of heroes, but the list would be too long for this one book; however, I would like to mention one other person, Dr. Sanford Wright Jr. of Everett, Washington who has been a hero in my life and in the lives of so many.

In addition to the many lives that he has touched through his medical career as an outstanding neurosurgeon, the world of the arts, specifically music and dance, has greatly benefited from his passion, dedication and his tremendous philanthropic contributions.

Additionally, Sanford's wife, Olga Foraponova Wright, is a two-time U.S. Ballroom Dance Champion and World Show-dance finalist and a hero to many young, aspiring dancers.

So many of their contributions are undocumented, but everyone who knows Sanford and Olga know of their love of people and their commitment to making a difference in the world.

Dr. Wright's strong support of the Everett chapter of the Volunteers of America birthed an annual Christmas celebration extravaganza, *A Christmas Spectacular,* which ran for over 20 years. This show was extremely popular in the Seattle and Everett communities and featured talent from all over the world.

Dr. Wright gives generously to a number of charities. As I mentioned before, so many of Sanford's acts of kindness and philanthropy are undocumented, but I'm sure, are no less appreciated.

He mentioned to me once that the joy that he receives back from giving to others is priceless and his acts of giving keeps him feeling happy and fulfilled. When we give to others as an act of love, all of that love and goodness is returned to us.

Presently, Dr. Wright has established a new organization, Monumental Talks, which highlights the success stories of immigrants and refugees to the United States and the benefits they received through and because of this great nation. This program is in its infancy and we are excited about hearing more about Dr. Wright and Monumental Talks!

I encourage you to find the heroes in your world; on the job, in the community and make it a point to go out and to thank them for being a shining light, for expressing the beauty of life and for being an example of brotherly and sisterly love. Let them know that they are making a difference.

In every human heart, there is a spark of goodness. Each of us has the power to make a difference and to live each day, encouraging others. Decide today to make your life count by becoming someone's hero.

27

In the Silence – Part A

Sitting in the silence can be a hard thing to accomplish in today's busy world. Finding respite in our days, allowing moments of silence can be enormously beneficial.

In multiple studies it is found that people who practice silence on a regular basis have better health, greater peace, more energy and receive greater insights. The benefits of this practice are powerful and undeniable.

In Eastern cultures the practice of silence is far more predominant than here, in the West. It is effective in clarity of mind and in achieving excellence. Many martial arts disciplines make this a necessary part of the training to achieve the highest levels of proficiency.

One way to practice silence is to regularly allow time to be still, taking intervals throughout the day for our minds to rest. The mind is a powerful tool, but it can become fatigued from overuse and overstimulation.

Many years ago, I had the privilege of playing piano at a private reception for the Nordstrom corporation on the trading floor of the New York Stock Exchange. Just the pace of the city and the madness at the opening of the Exchange was overwhelming to me.

I had played a private reception for the event the night before and in the morning, Nordstrom executives gathered for the ringing of the bell to start the trading, as I performed piano music just before the ceremony.

Afterwards, some of the traders, brokers and workers commented to me that they wished I were playing music there every morning. They said that the music was so calming and soothing. It gave them peace.

A fast-paced, hectic atmosphere affects our nervous system on an unconscious level. It is important to balance this with daily intervals for quiet reflection.

We may not be in such a high-pressure environment as the New York Stock Exchange, but it is still important to maintain a balance and the benefits from the practice of silence are enormous.

For those new to this idea and would like to introduce periods of silence into their daily lives, can do so. One simple technique is focusing on the rhythm of your breath.

Our breath is the one thing that is constant and that we utilize consistently throughout our entire lives. We can consciously use this as a tool for centering ourselves and for calming the mind. Focusing on the breath is simply giving our minds something to focus on, as a means of calming our mental activity.

The practice is simple, as you sit in a still, quiet place, focus your attention on your breath. Don't try to control your breathing, just notice it, focus your mind on your breath (breathing: in… out… in… out… in… out…). Some people may find it helpful to count their breaths during this exercise.

As your thoughts begin to drift away from the breath, just gently return to focusing on the breath. As many times as your thoughts drift, gently return your focus to your breath. Don't be upset that your mind drifted, just return to your breathing. It is not possible to stop the mind from thinking. With practice in silence, over time you can gradually begin to quiet your mind more effectively.

As you practice this for a few days you will notice that you have more energy and clearer thinking. I suggest doing this practice daily, for 10-20 minutes at a time. You can vary the amount of time as best suits you. You will discover great benefits from this simple practice.

As stated earlier, one of the most amazing benefits of this practice is mental clarity and an increased intuition. As a result, you will find new answers and insights.

One thing to note is that these insights may not come while sitting in the silence. They will generally show up at a time when we're not expecting it. Don't look for results. The results will be self-evident.

Stilling our minds is important. It allows us to recenter. So often we become lost in our thoughts and hardly even notice the world around us.

Sometimes we may not have the proper time to sit in the silence. In this case, I would suggest another tool for calming the mind. This is the practice of awareness, or mindfulness.

While sitting or walking simply notice the things around you, purposely looking at the details of things in your environment. Notice your breath, though not focusing on it, with your eyes open, set your attention on being *present* in your thoughts, as you observe the world around you. It is important to have no judgements during this exercise, only an observance. As you become more *present* your thoughts will calm down.

Another way to use this practice is to employ other senses, for example sometimes while walking I may choose to focus on the sense of sound and listen to detect all of the distinct sounds in my environment, or I may focus on the sense of smell or touch. In so doing, I immediately calm my mind and begin to actually appreciate the world around me.

This practice of awareness has the same effect as sitting in the silence, which calms the mind and brings my thoughts to the present. It gets me out of my head.

Walking in nature is a perfect time to become immersed in allowing all of your senses to be awakened and aware. This practice is centering, it is both calming and healing.

27

In the Silence – Part B

As mentioned above, the practice of silence enhances intuition. An important step in receiving answers is to ask questions. It is amazing how we receive the answers when we ask. I have discovered many answers this way and the more questions I ask, the more insights I receive.

When I say to ask questions, I do not mean to ask another person, but I mean to verbalize questions to yourself. Perhaps this may sound odd, to ask questions of ourselves, however, consider this; the majority of the functions which go on in our bodies are involuntary and are governed by a vast intelligence beyond our comprehension or understanding.

In fact, estimates say that 90 percent of our bodily functions are involuntary and are carried out by the *subconscious mind.* So then, our conscious mind is only providing us about 10% of accessible knowledge.

The heart is an organ that operates involuntarily and is working 24 hours a day, 7 days a week, year after year, throughout our entire lives, pumping blood through the 60,000 miles of blood vessels in our bodies, even while we are asleep. Most of the time we are not even aware of this amazing, essential, continuous function.

Our breath is sustained involuntarily, as our lungs expand and contract in a continuous, perfectly orchestrated rhythm. Both the heart and the lungs vary their rhythm based on the conditions of our actions and environment.

When we get a scratch on our skin, the body goes to work to arrest the blood flow and then immediately calls in the "repair team" to go to work to repair the damage, sealing the wound.

When a foreign substance enters the body, specialized patrol cells detect the intruder. These cells extract the intruder's contents and carry it off to be analyzed.

This information is interpreted by the brain's endless catalogues of information, to find a match for the type of intruder. When a match is discovered, immediately white blood cells and other necessary agents are ordered to go to work to subdue the intruder.

Wouldn't it make sense that if we have questions or are in need of a healing in our bodies, to consider enquiring of this vast intelligence which already knows how to heal the body and how to govern every system within us?

The digestive and elimination systems of the body operate without our knowledge, dissolving, assimilating and distributing essential nutrients all throughout our bodies to nourish our one hundred trillion cells, to build muscle, bone, tissue, supplying our glands with the essential elements for the production of and the secretion of hormones, enzymes and millions of cellular functions, every second of our lives, working continuously to keep us alive. And this all takes place beneath our level of consciousness. Even our sense organs operate automatically, serving us day and night, recording every detail of our life story.

There are endless, daily agendas of functions administered throughout our bodies which our conscious minds have no knowledge of. This is but a short list of a few of the involuntary responses of our amazing bodies!

Imagine the number of timed, necessary functions, on a cellular level, that go on in a woman's body to produce a baby!! To our conscious minds this would be inconceivable, but to our subconscious minds it takes place effortlessly.

This vast world is operating within us continually, standing guard, poised at any instant to deploy whatever operation is necessary at any given moment to sustain our lives. The intelligence which governs these systems, is a wisdom which will provide us answers when we ask questions.

The subconscious mind never sleeps and is functioning our entire lives. Yes, we really are more magnificent than we could ever conceive!

Our bodies house a natural "pharmacy", complete with pain killers, sedatives, and many other naturally dispensed drugs. Here is an excerpt from an article in the Chicago Tribune entitled, "The Body Pharmacy"

The body's pharmacy offers natural pain killers as potent as morphine, sleeping aids, medicines for stroke and heart attack victims-even what may prove to be the world's long-sought aphrodisiac.

Cancer treatment is one major front where these types of drugs hold promise.

Our bodies are supplied with a storehouse of natural remedies for a plethora of conditions and symptoms. A fully stocked internal pharmacy! The article continues…

Genentech, the California-based genetic engineering firm, has found a family of drugs in the body's own immune system that selectively destroys cancer cells.

The company expects to market gamma interferon, a more well-known anti-cancer drug also discovered in the immune system, in 1986 or 1987.

So just how do we go about accessing these internal drugs? Every cell in our bodies responds to our feelings, our thoughts and everything that we say. Yes, it's true that every thought or emotion affects *every cell in our bodies*. Many of these messages are received internally as "commands" and in many cases, as was discussed in a previous chapter, can improve or diminish our health based on the nature of these messages.

We need to understand that there are many factors which can contribute to illness and there are no easy answers. I am not a doctor, nor do I offer any medical advice. My advice is to seek the advice of a medical professional when dealing with an illness. However, understanding the fact that there are natural defenses within us to aid us, can be greatly beneficial and can offer us hope of recovery.

Our bodies maintain a delicate balance in keeping us healthy. Negative moods and emotions affect our body's responses to a marked degree and actually alter our body's metabolism in a variety of ways: increasing or diminishing heart rate, affecting blood pressure, causing our breathing to become shallow, or drastically increased during fits of anger, secretions of stress hormones into the bloodstream and other cellular reactions occur, altering our body's metabolic stability, which in turn affects our health.

It is a known fact that living in prolonged, stressful states act upon our bodies and minds negatively, weakening the immune system and are contributing factors in illness and disease.

It would seem to me that toxic feelings, toxic thinking and toxic speech may contribute to toxicity in the cells of our bodies which could adversely affect our health. This being the case, the practice of positivity in speech, feelings and thoughts will assist us in the *direction* of health and wholeness.

While it's true that we may not be able to control the state of our health during illness, it is important to understand the part that we *can* play in assisting our bodies towards the *direction* of health and wellness and perhaps assist in accessing our body's own natural defenses, stored within our internal "pharmacy."

Positive thoughts, positive conversations and a positive environment create an atmosphere of minimal resistance which can assist us in allowing our bodies to use our energy to focus on healing and recovery, instead of battling with unnecessary negativity, hostility and distractions.

27

In the Silence – Part C

As mentioned previously, another aspect of our subconscious mind is its intuitive sense. It is this part of our minds which encompasses our dreams, during sleep.

Many times we receive messages and answers while asleep or in a meditative state. When we ask ourselves questions, we access this intuition and gain answers to life's perplexing questions.

Sometimes the answers may come to us as a passing thought, sometimes through another person, sometimes through a sign we read, in a book or a message or sometimes in a dream. Sometimes we will just know the answer.

The more that we open ourselves up to *listening* to our inner selves, the more of these hidden secrets will be revealed to us. Our moments of silence open us up to receive information from this vast storehouse.

Sometimes we may receive information on something that is in the future, a premonition of things to come, or we may be informed of something of which our conscious minds have no knowledge.

We have all had the experience of knowing that someone was staring at us without any conscious way of knowing that this was the case. As we look around, we see that our intuition was correct as we lock eyes with a person staring right at us. But how did we know that someone was staring at us in the first place?

In light of these facts, it becomes very clear that there is a Higher Intelligence, to which we are connected and are able to access information. The amount of information that we can access is based on our openness to this idea of accessing information intuitively, our level of awareness and on the development of our intuitive abilities.

The beauty of accessing this incredible storehouse of information from within, is that we can ask any kinds of questions and receive answers. Sometimes I have asked questions and didn't receive an answer. I then changed the *way* that I asked the question and then received the answer.

When asking questions be sure to ask empowering questions. A question like, "Why do bad things happen to me?" is not an empowered question, is too vague and will not be answered. We must be *specific* and *clear* in what we are seeking an answer to.

The best part about this is that we don't have to add anything to ourselves to access this amazing tool, it's already a part of who we are and has been with us our entire lives.

Also, the synchronicities of life events may not be just random events but are sometimes the universe trying to tell us something. I have experienced this in my own life. My wife mentioned to me the importance of reaching out to people right away, who come to your mind. She said that the fact that we thought of them may be more significant than we may realize.

I have followed this advice and have had a number of extremely significant connections with individuals that I had not spoken to for decades, who were in trouble, or others who were trying to reach out to me. I have been amazed that the timing of my response was profoundly significant to the effectiveness of these encounters.

Additionally, if we find ourselves constantly bumping into things, tripping and bumping our heads, this might be a good time to ask the question, "Why does this keep happening to me? What is the message to me?"

It is vitally important to ask questions, because we can sometimes easily misinterpret a situation, not understanding the underlying message.

Sometimes I have asked questions and later read a billboard or a sign on a bus or heard something in a conversation of strangers and realized that this was the answer to my question.

The more that we learn to be silent and to tune into this intelligent life Force, the same Force which is in every living thing and that which governs the universe, the more our lives will harmonize, balance and flow with the easy flow of nature and the universe.

Give the practices of silence and mindfulness a try for a few weeks. These are great tools for developing personal mastery. The possibilities from developing this practice are vast and life changing. I believe that you will find, as I have, that the rewards from the practice of silence and of awareness are invaluable.

28

Happiness Keys

One of the greatest pursuits in life is the quest to find sustained happiness. The vital first step in acquiring this virtue is to make the decision to be happy. The decision to be happy changes our perspective, allowing us to see the beauty which *already is.* Appreciating the beauty that is already abundant around us can bring us a degree of happiness.

To add to this thought we can find beauty and a lifting of our spirits through the beauty in nature and through the arts. Nature's power to heal and rejuvenate is unmatched. To spend time in its magical embrace is to welcome more peace and joy into our lives.

For instance, just taking time to watch squirrels playing, tumbling in the grass, or children at play can't help but bring a smile. Sitting beside a body of water has a tremendous calming effect, as we relax and watch the waves in motion or meditate on the calm, still waters.

Nature also provides us with unmatched beauty in its trees, plants and flowers. There are an endless number of things to explore in nature, all of which refresh and rejuvenate the mind, body and soul.

I love flowers. I feel that these are a reminder to us of the constant beauty that underlies every moment. Flowers are so simple, yet so profound. Taking the time to actually see them, to experience them and to "drink" in their beauty and grace can be rejuvenating and enormously gratifying.

Music, art, poetry, dance and other artistic expressions can also stimulate our senses and bring more beauty to our lives and in turn invite happiness. Obviously, some art forms and musical styles are better than others for achieving this purpose.

There are many other things which tend to happiness. Jerry Jampolski, in his book, Love Is Letting Go of Fear, suggests that the act of giving to others, those things which we would want for ourselves, is a way to obtain peace and happiness. This means that if we want to receive love, we must first show love to others. If we want goodness, we must share goodness and if we want to be happy, we must do things which make others happy.

Giving to others in a purely altruistic way is a sure way to acquire greater happiness. In fact, I have discovered that if we live our lives by this principle, we can have a greater degree of sustained happiness.

One way to give love is to practice, throughout the day, greeting people as you pass them and to share a compliment; "Love the dress!", "What a beautiful hat!", "You have a lovely smile!", "That's a sharp pair of shoes." These kinds of selfless acts not only lift the person we're speaking to but in turn will lift us and bring a smile to our faces as we extend love and kindness.

One day while having lunch at work, I smiled at a woman as she passed my table. She went a short distance and then turned and came back to me. She said to me, "You don't know what that smile did for me. I really needed that!" It was clear to me that she had been going through a tough time and my smile was just the medicine to lift her spirit.

One smile can make all the difference. The beautiful part about this, is that a smile doesn't cost us anything. It's just a simple acknowledgment that says, "I notice you and I wish you well." It's a simple gesture that can go a long way. We never know what effect we're having on other people through our simple acts of kindness.

Being grateful is another way to obtain joy, when we express our appreciation for life's many gifts.

Offering help for someone in need or giving monetary assistance, are also ways that we can bring more happiness into our lives. Receiving assistance when we are in need is certainly a wonderful thing, but when we are in the position of giving to others, and we give, unconditionally, out of the goodness of our hearts, this returns joy to us. The quickest way to bring more happiness into our lives is to first, get out of ourselves and to extend love to someone else.

This idea is often seen at Christmas time. The person who has bought a special gift and wrapped it with care, sits in excited anticipation of the opening of the beautifully wrapped package. The joy and delight that comes to the *giver* is often equal to, or sometimes even greater than the joy of the person receiving the gift! The joy that comes from unconditional giving is quickly returned to the giver in abundant measure.

To find more joy in living, *never* miss an opportunity to *give* to those you love at birthdays and holidays. Why? Because this is one sure way to fill up *your* love tank!

If we are focused solely on ourselves in life and are not sharing with others, we unknowingly are robbing ourselves of the gifts of happiness that can only come through sharing. Don't get me wrong, there are many ways to obtain happiness, but I have found that the happiness that I have experienced, which has come as a result of my giving from a heart of love to others, is more rewarding and is more sustaining than the happiness I have experienced by other means.

Whenever I have touched someone else through an act of kindness, I smile just at the memory of the good deed, long afterwards. It's not about what you receive, but it's what you give away that counts.

Perhaps this is so rewarding, because this is the combined effects of the *love* in the action of the giver, with the *joy* in the heart of the receiver, making it twice as rewarding as anything would be which only benefits us.

Unfortunately, many people are not aware of this riddle of life and instead live their lives focused only on their own needs and wants, neglecting to share. As a consequence, they feel left out, as one sitting on the sidelines of life, watching the world drift past their window, wondering why they are so unhappy. How sad.

This principle of giving works, not because it is a good suggestion, but because it is based on universal laws. Take this advice, get out of your own way, develop the giving habit and enjoy the happiness it brings!

For those who may struggle with giving, know that it's really not that diffi-cult to do. Just do it! If money is an issue in giving a gift, then make something to offer as a gift. Be creative.

There are certainly other things we can give other than money. As men-tioned earlier we can give encouraging words, we can give of our time, we can give flowers, make a card, give a helping hand, etc. It's more about the act of giving than anything else.

The rewards that *you* receive back from a life of giving and sharing will be well worth the effort. You will feel good in your heart, knowing that you are making a difference for someone else. This is a path to greater happiness, guaranteed!

This principle of receiving the gift of happiness in return, through our giving from a heart of love and kindness is supported by both, the law of cause and effect and the law of attraction. Cause and effect is activated; "To every action there is a corresponding reaction." If there is no initial action, or cause, there will be no reaction. This law is activated by action. This is how the *giver* initiates this law.

The law of attraction also supports this as this law is based on, the good that we give out is returned to us or is attracted back to us. It may come back from somewhere completely unrelated to the original person, time or location, but nevertheless it will return back to the sender.

Do not give expecting anything back, because this is not giving out of love, but from some other motive and whatever is the underlying motive will attract back to the giver more of the same. One way to avoid this is to sometimes give to someone who is not able to return anything to you. In this case the act of benevolence is done out of a pure heart of love, care and empathy.

Some people try to find the cheapest things to give away, but don't realize that in doing so they are simply robbing themselves, missing an important opportunity and are missing the point of the act of giving. Plus, this is sending a bad message to the receiver.

What we give to others we are really giving to ourselves. If the giving can-not be done from a motive of pure love, then it's best not to do it at all. Giving from a heart of love and joy is the right way to give and will return to those who give, the gifts of joy and happiness.

If you are unable to give anything materially, then give your love, a smile, your support, a helping hand. To live a life of continually extending love to others, is to live a life of sustained joy and happiness.

I would like to add one cautionary note, beware of giving to the same individuals repeatedly, unless you have a good reason for doing so. In some cases, if we're not aware we may be enabling someone and not really helping them at all. And I find that giving to people who are ungrateful is also something that I try to avoid.

Each day we have a certain amount of love and goodness that we can share with others. If we don't share the love that we have, it will simply be depleted, wasted. If we liberally share our love, it will be returned to us and we will continue to be refilled; we now have that much more love and goodness to give away and in turn we receive the gift of love and happiness.

There is a verse from a song by Oscar Hammerstein from the musical, The Sound of Music that I feel sums this up nicely,

"A bell's not a bell 'til you ring it, A song's not a song 'til you sing it. The love in your heart wasn't put there to stay. Love isn't love until you give it away."

Living a life spreading joy, love and happiness is a sure way to fill our love tanks, making us a source of goodness and at the same time, returning to us joy and sustained happiness.

29

The Riddle of Life

What we feel about ourselves determines our world, our future. If we don't genuinely have a good opinion of ourselves, we cannot be truly happy and this will taint our lives and our relationships. It is vital that we develop a positive self-acceptance.

Outer circumstances are determined by inner states. If you want to change your life, focus on yourself. So, what is the riddle of life? One of the riddles in life is the knowledge that the key to the answers we are seeking is to be found by going within ourselves.

Our self-image is the seat of all that pertains to us and our world. The keys to our change in circumstances are locked within us, within our self-image.

The self-image (the way that I see myself) determines everything in our lives. It determines the limits of how high or how low we go. It determines the parameters of our entire existence.

For those of us who live in the city we have all seen the man on the corner, asking for money. He waits at the stop light and approaches the cars.

Some of these individuals carry a sign, for instance, the sign may read, "25¢." The person holding the sign may not realize it, but this is the value that this individual has placed upon himself. This becomes the worth of the individual, according to their own estimation. Not that a human being is only worth a quarter, but our belief in our own worth becomes the standard by which all things in our lives are measured.

The circumstances and the events of our lives are a *reflection,* mirroring back to us that which we define ourselves to be. The individual holding the "25¢" sign is trapped in a world of limited possibilities.

The truth of this fact is astonishing. It is because of this fact that a person starting out in life at the very bottom can eventually climb to unparalleled heights.

And conversely, an individual can also plummet from great heights to incredible depths by this same unavoidable truth, that a large part of our world is determined by our thoughts, words, beliefs, feelings and actions. Our outer states and circumstances are determined by and reflect our inner states. In order to alter our outer circumstances we must make the change internally. This is one of the great riddles of life.

Whether we realize it or not, everyone of us is "holding a sign", like the man on the corner. Every day, everyone of us carries a value that we have placed upon ourselves and everything in our life is determined by this invisible value system, our own self-worth, our self-image. So, what does your sign read? Or put another way, "What am I saying to myself, about myself?"

This is the case even if our beliefs are not actually true or are not based on facts. What we identify with becomes *our* truth.

My sister Belinda says that we all view our lives through a "lens". This lens "colors" or distorts our view. This distortion could be the result of events from our past which cloud our present view of life and may prevent us from seeing the truth of things as they truly are.

Our own self-assessment not only determines our lives, but this also determines other people's estimation of us. Their estimate of us *is* the estimate we hold of ourselves. If we hold a low regard for ourselves, then others will have little regard for us. Even if there is an attempt at promotion, the negative self-image will cause us to sabotage this promotion in some way.

Conversely, if we hold ourselves in high esteem, then others will respect us and hold us in high esteem. Even if a person is not liked, they will still be respected, because they have a high regard for themselves.

This, however, is not the same as having a big ego. Being egotistical is often a coverup for true feelings of inadequacy and this put-on behavior may be a disguise. A truly confident person has nothing to prove.

Having real self-confidence gives off a feeling of self-assurance and security in ourselves which translates to others, a belief in us. This personal assurance makes it easy for others to believe in us, because we believe in ourselves.

Everything in the universe has a vibration, a frequency, and the same is true for every person. Every person radiates energy and people feel this vibration from us. Some people have a weak vibration while others radiate power and esteem. For example, former President Ronald Reagan radiated confidence and power and this energy is a large part of how he was able to live such a dynamic life.

The beautiful part about this idea is that we can change our energy, our vibration, by changing our thoughts, our words and more importantly our *feelings*. Again, it goes back to what we believe about ourselves and the words we say to ourselves.

The key to transformation is to gain an inner confidence and a belief in ourselves on a *subconscious level*. Forming a vision of our *best self*, as well as learning to live in an expectation of good things and higher ideals will put us on the path to greater success in life.

Some people feel bad about themselves, and some are ashamed of themselves for their past sins and misdeeds. A sense of guilt and shame can cripple our lives and cause a continual stagnation. Though we try to climb up the ladder, we are continually held back and pulled down by our own negative self-perceptions and emotions.

An interesting perspective on this is presented in the book, The Untethered Soul, by Michael A. Singer, in which the author reveals the fact that indeed, we are *not* our thoughts, nor are we our emotions. This is not to say that we are not to be held accountable for our deeds, but it does reveal a profound universal truth.

It is true that we all have continuous thought narratives with ourselves, which go on in our minds. This is how the mind works. In the book, the author mentions these continuous streams of words in our minds and then asks the question, "Who is speaking to whom? Who is the one speaking? Who is the one listening to these thoughts? Who is the one feeling these emotions?" When asking these questions it becomes clear that there is a "self" beyond the thinking mind.

This person, or our true self, our core essence is pure conscious awareness. This is the one who simply observes and is the essence of who we are. This essence never speaks, is never sick, never has been sick, has no opinions or judgments, it simply *is*. This is the "self" beyond the ego.

This is the essence, the *life* within every living thing and within each one of us; our real self; the awareness of being. Some people referred to this part of us as our subconscious mind.

The more that we learn to quiet our minds, the more we'll begin to recognize and to live our lives from our center, from this vital life force within ourselves.

Yes, the truth that we are not our thoughts is further supported by the fact that we don't respond to every thought that crosses our minds.

It is a fact that the average person thinks thousands of thoughts every day. All of us have had thoughts which are fanciful and sometimes ridiculous, for example, a stray thought that we can fly. Fortunately, our rational mind governs and decides whether or not this thought is useful and needs to be acted upon, or to be discarded.

This awareness within us has a primary function of the preservation of life and can be useful in guiding us in the direction of our goals and our destinies.

We have the ability to override this intelligence, as many people do, and it is apparent that many people are unaware of this knowledge and therefore unable to benefit from it. Our lives will harmonize as we slow down and view our lives from this quite center. The practice of mindfulness allows us to live our lives from this centered place.

Currently, I am employed at Houston Methodist Hospital, voted as the Number One hospital in Texas. During the Covid 19 pandemic, Methodist offered a number of programs encouraging its employees to practice mindfulness meditation regularly, as a means of re-centering, as we coped with the increased stresses due to the effects of the pandemic. Both before and after the pandemic, Houston Methodist has, and continues to promote these programs for greater happiness and emotional wellbeing, as the stresses of working in healthcare can be overwhelming.

Mindfulness meditation puts us directly in touch with this core "self" and allows us a simple path to greater ease and greater focus. The more that we identify with this part of ourselves, the more ease and beauty we will express.

Our thinking, conscious, ego-mind can be filled with wrong information and if we are directed solely by this, we can certainly understand why the world is in such a state! Understanding that we are not our thoughts and understanding this principle of our true essence allows us to free ourselves from destructive thought patterns and to begin to recognize our true worth. Learning to "silence the chatter" and to live life from our center is the first step towards personal mastery.

Having the understanding of this truth, we can begin to measure our worth according to the beauty of our core essence and not rate ourselves, based solely on what we do. It's more about *who* we are than *what* we do.

With this approach to life, we will become more effective and efficient and can free ourselves from the confines of our thoughts and gain insights and strength from our center.

One of the riddles of life then, is having the understanding that the answers I seek are buried within me and as I become better acquainted with myself, this real truth of me, I can thereby discover answers to these hidden secrets and begin to express my full potential.

Each new day is a new opportunity to "write the book" or establish our own personal constitution on who we are, through which we can begin to guide our lives in the direction of our dreams and our desires.

30

Just in Case

Our society has checks and balances for things that are most important to us. Insurance is an institution established for this very purpose. We have health insurance, dental insurance, auto insurance, life insurance, flood insurance, homeowners' insurance and other types of insurance to help in giving us a sense of security.

What if there was a way to secure our future in the hereafter, or at least a way to find answers to life's greatest mystery?

The person that secures adequate insurance is not only seen as responsible, wise and acceptable but this has become the standard in our society. I would agree that the person who doesn't just leave this greatest of questions to chance is indeed a wise individual.

Because of the certainty of life and death and because of the finality of death, we cannot find any consolation in that final pronouncement. Working in a hospital setting I see it all the time as countless people are forced to confront this unwanted reality.

So many people are content to live their lives ignoring this fact of life. Society is ignoring "the elephant in the room" or is putting out of their minds the thought of death and in the hereafter.

The truth is that we are all wearing an "expiration tag" and the inevitable will eventually present itself. Perhaps we might find greater consolation in gaining a greater insight, through discovering the answers to these questions before we are presented with them.

Many times, I have observed one common denominator when this issue becomes a reality in our lives. I find people turning to something bigger than themselves. I find them in the chapel, seeking strength and guidance to questions that cannot be answered any other way.

Another thing that I've observed is that some people hold a grudge for a lifetime and then when faced with the end, see the importance of forgiving others, righting the wrongs of the past before transitioning. Why not live a life of forgiveness and instead of living those wasted years holding a grudge, learn to forgive and thereby enjoy more of life's goodness and loving relationships, presently? Life is full of so much beauty when we unload our excess baggage.

As an interesting side note, when I was in high school, I had a discussion with a fellow student on the origins of life. They came from the perspective of evolution while I spoke of creation.

I asked, "Where did man come from?" They answered, "From apes." I then asked, "Where did the apes come from?" "From fish." I then asked the question, "Where did life come from?" Their answer was, "From one-celled organisms." My response was, "Who gave life to the one-celled organisms?" There was a long silence. That marked the end of our discussion.

At one time in my life, I questioned the purpose of life and sought to know the truth of my existence. I decided that instead of leaving this most important question to chance or to someone's opinion, I would simply ask the Source!

I prayed and asked if there were anyone listening who might shed some light on this. I didn't want anyone's opinions or theories. Specifically, I prayed, "There are so many different churches, religions and teachings in the world on what is truth and what is right and it is obvious to me that not all of these views are true. I don't want to live a lifetime and then discover at the end that I was all wrong."

I then began to ask to be shown the truth. I prayed, "What is the truth? Show me the truth. Show me the truth. I want to know the truth." I sought an answer earnestly for a few days. I was determined to get an answer.

I was pleasantly surprised to receive an answer and insight into what was necessary for me to do. I received guidance and an answer to my question.

When we consider this universe with its billions of stars and galaxies, it is clear that for anyone to piously think that they have all the answers and that they've got it all figured out is not only being presumptuous, but downright absurd! The only one that *does* have the answer to these questions is the One that created it!

I now make prayer a regular part of my life and have found the answers to many questions this way. In fact, when I considered writing this book, I sought guidance on this, which I received. I later received guidance on including this specific chapter. Personally, I was going to leave it out, but after receiving instructions to include it, I decided to leave it in.

One thing I have noticed in asking questions in prayer, is that I must be *earnest* in my request, *specific* in my questions and I must *wait* for the answers. If I need more clarity, I just ask again. The Source, which is the intelligence of the entire universe, is infinite, inexhaustible. Yes, we can find answers to our perplexing questions.

I now find many answers through seeking truth, not according to opinions or what I might feel, but I seek the *Wisdom* which has established and governs this universe. I have found this to be the best "life insurance policy."

I am not here to tell anyone what I feel that they should do but I do know that there is a place that we can go to find the answers to any situation regarding this life and the hereafter. We have a right to know.

I think the greatest "insurance policy" that we can possess, which brings the greatest assurance, is establishing a relationship with the Source of life and having the comfort of being guided by this wisdom, which has established and governs all life in the universe.

While we are living on this side of life, we have the power and the right of choice. It is one of our greatest gifts, our greatest liberty. When we cross over to the other side, into the unknown, we will be solely at the mercy of that which lies beyond, and our choices will be determined by forces beyond our control. Understanding that this day of our transitioning is eminent, I think it might be a good idea to have our "insurance plan" established and in place before our departure.

When I come to the place that I have completed my course here on earth and am facing my end, the one thing that will matter the most will be the assurance that I have settled my business beforehand. If there is a purpose to my being here, I want to make sure that I have completed it while I am here. After I'm gone there will be no *do overs*.

There's an old song that talks about riding a train to glory. Just in case I need a "ticket" to ride this train or to have completed some specific "rite of passage" to enter this next phase of life, it's my responsibility to make sure I've got this in place. One thing is for certain, it will be better to have it and not need it, then to need it and not have it!

31

Doing the "Think-Thunk"

When I was a child my brothers, sisters and I used to make up words and phrases. One of the phrases we created was "Doing the think-thunk." "Doing the think-thunk" is presuming what someone is thinking and then acting on that assumption. Needless to say, this produces a lot of unnecessary confusion.

I have discovered that this often happens in marriages and in relationships. Recently I had a situation where my wife was trying to be helpful to me with her advice, which I interpreted in a negative way. I felt as though she was trying to mother me or control me, and this led to an argument. This was solely based on my "think-thunking" what her intentions were. When she confided to me that her motive was love and helpfulness I had to apologize, realizing that I had overreacted.

Also in relationships, we sometimes fail to see the real person due to layers and layers and years and years of conditioning which may have blocked the view of the true person beneath the exterior.

One perspective which can be helpful in allowing us to see the true person, can be to imagine the person as a child. This inner child is alive and active in every person, no matter their age, and this child, though disguised, is still soft, vulnerable and yearning for the things that everyone of us desires; to be loved and accepted.

We are all basically the same and consequently are all plagued with the same fears, doubts and insecurities. If we take a moment to stop and see the inner child in an individual, we can perhaps connect more with the truth of the person that is within, beneath the surface.

It can also be insightful to do this exercise on ourselves, asking questions of the "child" within us. Behaviors in our adult lives can sometimes be traced back to our childhood. Revisiting this part of who we are may help us in solving questions in our adult life, taking us to the root of the problem.

Seeing things with a fresh perspective, may be helpful in allowing us to see the truth of the person within and perhaps may even allow us to replace our perspective with one that is more beneficial.

In an effort to practice clearer perception in relationships, we can clearly see how "doing the think-thunk" can create many problems. An extreme case of "think-thunking" is passing judgment...

While judging may be useful in some situations, we need to be careful not to become *overly* critical and judgmental. A judgmental habit can influence our attitudes and undermine our own happiness.

Obviously using sound judgment can be very important and, in some situations, may even be vital to our survival. Certainly, we understand the importance of exercising judgment in character. Living in a big city it is wise to practice some restraint in dealings with strangers. However, it wouldn't be wise to make a habit of *pre-judging* every situation negatively, as we may misperceive some situations and in doing so, may miss the truth.

Overly negative, judgmental habits can cloud the truth, preventing us from seeing things as they truly are. Truth and clarity come from actually seeing things, without judgements. Sometimes when the truth is revealed we may discover that our preconceived notions were entirely wrong.

To gain a better perspective it may be useful to learn to view life objectively, without judgements. The practice of mindfulness is this very practice; of seeing things without judgements. In so doing, we will discover more beauty which is sometimes closer than we may think.

Experiences which are meant to be beautiful can sometimes be negatively affected by an overly critical, judgmental perspective, clouding the beauty right before us. Unbiased perception yields the beauty in the present moment.

Judgmental prejudices produce a vision of distortion, which is not capable of seeing clearly, until the judgements are put aside.

At times I have found myself guilty of being overly judgmental and would have missed the beauty in many situations, had I not caught myself and instead, focused on being in the moment, and enjoying the experience, non-judgmentally. Being overly critical may rob us of the enjoyment of many beautiful experiences.

Learning to put aside judgements takes practice, as it is our tendency as humans, and especially in our society, to quickly assess situations and to put forth a judgment. In this age of social media where everyone freely expresses their opinions and their viewpoints it is easy to become swayed and sometimes adopt a viewpoint which may be heavily influenced and perhaps, may not necessarily be our own thoughts or opinions.

Some of the greatest individuals in history were labeled in terms which were polar opposites. Consider this; Lao Tzu, Jesus, The Buddha, Grigori Rasputin, Mahatma Gandhi, the Apostle Paul, Mother Teresa, Saint Francis of Assisi and many of the Greek Philosophers were seen by some as the Messiah, the Enlightened One, as saints, wise men and women, healers and even as the saviors of the world, while others saw these same individuals as heretics, phonies, traitors, devils, charlatans, witches and quacks.

Many of these judgements were based on *here-say* and swayed the opinions of the masses. They certainly couldn't be *both* at the same time! Obviously, in some cases these individuals were defined through the eyes of distortion and condemnation, certainly not through the eyes of truth.

I'm not saying that I necessarily embrace all of the teachings of these individuals mentioned here, nor am I saying that I believe in or follow their doctrines, but what I am saying is that each one of them cast a broad range of influence over multitudes, while having as many followers as those who opposed their teachings. It can be difficult to know what's true while judging purely on appearances.

Here's an interesting thought, suppose we had lived during the time period of one or more of these individuals and had had a personal encountered with them. What would our assessment have been? Would we have seen them as enlightened, or would we have been one of their opponents bringing railing accusations and condemnation? Certainly, something to ponder.

A closed mind is incapable of perceiving higher levels of truth, because these levels are only accessible to an open mind. While the closed mind remains fixed in its judgments, it is incapable of seeing past the distortion.

The irony of truth, as revealed in the lives of the individuals mentioned above, is that profound truth is often shrouded in great controversy. Truth, though obscured and buried beneath a barrage of scrutiny, is no less true because of controversy.

Obviously, this is not the case of all controversy, nor would it be wise to assume that every controversial issue or figure is a bearer of truth, which would be an absurd notion, but historically, controversy has consistently, and continues to follow truth and the individuals that herald it.

Many people, unaware of this great fact, choose to see controversy as a verification of the lack of the truth, thereby keeping the light of truth further hidden from those with closed minds. This is a great paradox, one of the riddles of life.

By now it should be clear to the readers that so much of what we believe to be true in life may actually be backwards to our way of thinking. Because of this fact, it might be advisable, that before we accept any gossip or negativity we might hear about anyone and run off with our views of "certainty" on what we consider to be the "facts", it might be a better idea not to "think-thunk" or gossip about anyone.

Gossip taints our hearts and can be very toxic. And remember that the law of attraction is always operating and returns back to *us* whatever *we* give out.

Until we know the facts of a situation from the person's own lips, as to its certainty or validity, we really do not know what is true, as there's always another side to every story. Personally, I have enough work to do with my own life, that I don't have time to get caught up in other people's views of someone.

Many times, as in the case of the individuals mentioned above, what people are saying and what the truth is are often two very different stories and no one can gain a clear perspective without understanding all of the facts. It's best to judge every person on your own terms and not by borrowed, second-hand information.

Learn to adopt a positive attitude and work at the practice of objective, non-judgmental perception, drop "think-thunking" and in doing so, may you discover a richer life that's more beautiful, purposeful and more fulfilling.

32

An Exercise in Empathy

Empathy is defined as: The ability to understand and share the feelings of another.

We live in a society where the majority of people are predominately focused on his or her own needs, wants and desires. Of course, there are exceptions to this rule, but basically this is the way of the world. Sometimes we can be so caught up in our own affairs that we can forget that there are other people around us who need our care and attention.

There is a saying, "We wouldn't worry so much what other people think of us when we realize how seldom they do." This about sums it up. People are not thinking about us as often as we may assume. Most of the time each person's thoughts are on his or her own world, problems, and affairs.

There's really nothing wrong with focusing on our own world and our issues, unless this is all we ever focus on. One thing to consider is that the more that we begin to direct our attention towards other people, the more fulfilling *our* lives become.

While this may be the case, there are some associations in life that may not be beneficial. In those cases, it might be advisable to detach from these associations and find a positive avenue for extending your love.

Learning to be more empathetic is an important issue and requires our attention, especially because we live in a very diverse society where it can be easy for certain groups of people to fall through the cracks. There are many people on the brink of breakdown who could be helped just by knowing that someone cares. Learn to live your life empathetically.

In the book, Search Inside Yourself by Chade-Meng Tan, an engineer at Google, offers an exercise for acquiring empathy, which can be helpful in facilitating this quality within us.

The exercise is to think of someone towards whom we would like to have good feelings. We might begin with those people closest to us and then move onto those more challenging relationships. As we do this exercise, it will help us to begin to see the person in a new light. Here is the exercise:

"Just Like Me"

"This person has a body and a mind, just like me.

This person has feelings, emotions, and thoughts, just like me.

This person has at some point in his or her life, been sad, disappointed, angry, hurt, or confused, just like me."

Through this exercise we can begin to realize that we are all the same and that we all have the same needs and desires. Through this process we can gain more empathy.

"This person has, in his or her life, experienced physical and emotional pain and suffering, just like me.

This person wishes to be free from pain and suffering, just like me.

This person wishes to be healthy and loved, and to have fulfilling relationships, just like me."

This exercise concludes with…

"This person wishes to be happy, just like me."

In practicing this method, we can begin to gain more empathy for others. Why is this important? Because empathy is one of our greatest human virtues. The more that we practice it, the more beauty is expressed through us.

Though it is true that *we, ourselves are* the most important person in our lives, we still need to realize that it's not about us all the time and in every circumstance. For instance, if someone is going through a serious illness and you "go off on them" for not calling you back when they said they would, or because they misplaced the television remote, perhaps you could be a bit more empathetic and make it more about what *they're* going through and less about your petty annoyances.

Sometimes we get our feelings hurt when others don't respond to us or act the way we would like. The truth is that sometimes people cannot be there for us, especially when they are going through a tough time, or are in a season where they find it hard to be there for themselves! Let's let people off the hook and give them the benefit of the doubt, presuming the best.

Finally practicing empathy is a choice and in acquiring this virtue in our lives we thereby lift others, while obtaining greater happiness and fulfillment for ourselves. The goodness that we extend to others is returned to us.

33

Dialing In

We have discussed in previous chapters, the importance of having quiet time, as a way of accessing information; to gain inner peace, insights and to find answers. Many people, religions and cultures believe in a Higher Intelligence which we all have the capability of accessing.

Some of the terms used for this Entity are God, the Universe, the Source, the Life Force, among many other names. While there is much division about the validity of such an entity and further division on just "Who?" or "What?" this entity might be, the evidence of the reality that "Someone", or "Something" must be responsible for the infinite, intricate complexities of creation and of life upon planet earth alone, let alone the infinite diversity of the universe, let's us know that creation certainly didn't just occur without any "rhyme or reason" and that the existence of mankind is not just some fluke of nature, of no consequence. With the evidence that surrounds us everywhere, our rational minds could not accept the futility of such a philosophy.

Connecting with this Entity is entirely possible and is available to every human being on planet earth. I would like to discuss two avenues for connecting with this Source, both of which are practiced throughout the world. One is through prayer and the other is through meditation.

In our world we find a great divide, which I feel is entirely unnecessary. Many people who advocate prayer, denounce meditation and see it as some form of sacrilege or as an occult practice, viewed in a negative light, while the world of meditators sometimes view those who pray as the "uninformed" and see them as being somehow lacking in understanding, in their "exaggerated" attempts to connect with Divinity.

Actually, I have discovered that both prayer and meditation are important factors in dealing with this Intelligence, and that they are not so far apart from each other.

Prayer, as practiced here in the West, is mainly seen as a way of "speaking" to God. The Bible uses verses which promote "asking", "making your requests known", "lifting up your voice", the Lord's Prayer, etc. With this approach, yes, we make our requests known, but too often, after we finish speaking, we get up, go our way and don't allow time to receive back any response. True prayer is meant to be a *communion,* a back-and-forth relationship with the Divine, making our requests known and then receiving back direction, comfort, and the gift of peace.

As I mentioned, our understanding of prayer is primarily about "speaking", while in meditation the main emphasis is on clearing our minds and "listening." In many forms of meditation there is no speech involved.

Some meditation practices teach that we should not ask for anything in prayer, as this Intelligence already knows our needs. While it is true that this Intelligence does know our thoughts and needs, nevertheless, I have found it good to make my requests known. Meditation is important because it allows us mental clarity to receive the quiet messages that are being relayed back to us.

I have found that the most effective way to connect with this Intelligence is through a combination of both of these approaches. I have received the greatest demonstrations from consistent prayer and from meditation, abiding in the presence of the Divine.

There are many forms of meditation. The type of meditation I practice and refer to is simply being quiet and still, while abiding in the Presence. Sometimes I may use my breath, an inspired thought or a scripture as a focal point in my meditations. Some meditation practices encourage chanting. I do not use chanting in my meditation practice.

In prayer, it is not necessary to use any special or formal language. I speak in prayer as I would speak with a friend. This Entity is wise and understands the thoughts of our hearts before we speak. Understand that when we connect with this Source, we are dealing with the most tremendous power in the universe.

Several years ago, I was searching for a solution to a personal problem. I was stressed out and worried for many days about the outcome. As I began to meditate on the presence of God, I heard these words clearly in my spirit, *"Haven't I always been there for you? Give it to me."* I immediately felt a peace come over me and knew that things were going to work out favorably. Though nothing had changed in my circumstances outwardly, these words encouraged me immeasurably, especially when I considered the Source!

Without having received this message I would have continued feeling stressed out. The peace that came from receiving this message was invaluable to me.

A few months later when I needed to have the solution in place, miraculously the answer came forth as promised, and the problem was solved in perfect time. I might add that during this season of my life I had made meditation a daily practice, which opened up my mind to receive this message.

I have had many, many answers to prayer and have developed an "ear" to receive messages from the Divine. Yes, prayer and meditation have many benefits and practical applications to everyday living.

There are many celebrities who practice prayer and meditation on a regular basis, who attribute their great successes to dialing into this Source. Here are just a few individuals who attribute their success to prayer and meditation and who practice this on a regular basis: Oprah Winfrey, Denzel Washington, Tyler Perry, Mark Wahlberg, Carrie Underwood, Tom Hanks, among countless others.

Sometimes when I am going through a difficult season, I will pray deep prayers. I have been amazed at the level of power that can be generated from these kinds of prayers. Though I find meditation to be very useful, I do not touch this depth within myself during meditation. It is for this reason that I advocate both prayer and meditation, using the right tools for the job.

One time I was seeking a miracle and had used visualization, affirmation and meditation, but did not receive a breakthrough. Then I prayed a very deep prayer, while visualizing a successful outcome and my answer came forth, speedily. This prayer was only a few minutes in length, but it touched a deep place within myself.

Another practice that generates power is through praise and thanksgiving to God for the goodness in our lives. Praise is a very powerful and effective tool for connecting with the Divine. There are tools for communing with this Life Force and through connecting with this tremendous power, miracles can and do happen!!

If you have not tried prayer as a method for finding answers or for greater efficiency, I would certainly recommend it. I am convinced that some life situations can *only* be solved through fervent prayers, making our requests known. It can also be effective to join with others in prayer for a particular matter, to be more effective.

Life is a continuous journey of learning as we go through a variety of challenges. Several years ago, I went through a situation where I was in need of a miracle and thought that I could do it on my own. I knew that there was power in prayer and I applied myself for several months, praying fervently, several times a day, with everything I could muster. No matter how I tried to receive a miracle, I failed in my attempt and learned a very hard lesson.

While I do believe in and have experienced many positive results through prayer and I know the necessity of connecting with this Power, sometimes we may not be equipped for dealing with certain situations. Understand that there are individuals who may be more experienced in the practice of prayer and sometimes it may be necessary to seek assistance in receiving an answer in prayer. Nevertheless, I do believe that the power of prayer can overcome any obstacles, as I mentioned before, we must use the right tools for the job.

Today, I join with the celebrities mentioned above and with those of us who know and have tested this power. I am convinced that to become my very best, I don't have to do it alone, but I can tap into infinite resources and gain strength from beyond, to overcome obstacles and find assistance to truly express my very best!

34

Make a Good Day!

When I would be out with my father and someone would greet him with the words, "Have a good day.", my father's response was, "No… MAKE a good day!" I like this philosophy, because it places the responsibility on us, individually, as to what kind of a day we determine to have.

Most of us base our opinions as to the kind of a day we're having on the events that happen around us and we, in-turn, interpret these experiences as the deciding factor as to what "sort of a day we're having." This becomes the basis for the way we choose to feel. With this approach we're giving our power away. With such an approach we are continually at the mercy of unpredictable circumstances beyond our control.

Let's suppose we determine to have a good day and then the events of our day are not going as we had hoped or anticipated. Now when asked by someone about our day our response is, "I'm not having such a good day." How can we better handle such a situation? Perhaps we can change our day simply by changing our perspective.

The entire premise behind my father's statement was to both, establish his positive position and also to challenge the other person to realize that they have greater power than they may realize.

So then, the first thing to consider in having a good day, is to *determine* that you're going to have the right attitude no matter what the day may bring.

With such a stance, you will not be so easily thrown off balance and you will learn not to sweat the small things.

Sometimes we can take things for granted and are so focused on yesterday or on tomorrow that we don't appreciate today. Then on other days we're so in our heads that we don't even notice the day at all!

Complaining can also be a factor which can taint our perspective and certainly we all can find things to complain about; however, it is important to replace complaints with gratitude for the things that are going right.

Personally, I make it a point in my day to stop and to name things for which I am grateful. This is a good practice to do in the morning, to start your day off right. In this way I am making gratitude a habit, a part of my regular thought process. In so doing, I change my outlook to the beauty and possibilities that are right in front of me.

Concerning gratitude, we can name literally hundreds of things for which we can be grateful. I practice beginning my day naming a long list of things for which I am grateful: being alive, waking up, food, clothing, good health, friends, and family, my car, living in the US, and so many other things to appreciate.

The more that I practice this, the better I feel, and I am thereby attracting more good things to myself. This is the best way to turn our days into good days. We certainly can't expect to receive more in life if we're not even grateful for what we already have.

"If the only prayer you say in your entire life is - 'Thank You'- that is enough."
- Meister Eckhart, 1260-1328

It is also a good practice to set out each day with a goal to positively affect someone's life that day. If you approach life this way, you will carry a smile, and an encouraging word; you will be courteous and neighborly; you will be helpful and loving, and life will become that much brighter, because sharing, loving and helping invites happiness.

As we expect goodness, look for the good in situations and in others, share goodness, speak goodness and practice goodness, it makes for an environment of goodness which spreads to others.

Even when things go terribly wrong, decide not to complain or get stressed, but rather to focus on whatever good there is and know that even storms come for a season and then eventually pass.

Keep hope alive at all times and keep your eye on helping others. With this way of living, you will never be empty, because through your kindness and a positive attitude, the goodness you give out will be returned to you.

Finally, in making any day into a good day, remember to take moments for yourself, where you do good things just for yourself. Sometimes when focused so much on doing for others, we can forget to do for ourselves. Practice being good to yourself.

Just doing simple things like taking a walk, smelling the roses along the way, visiting the spa, going for a swim or having a special dessert, anything that you enjoy doing and do it, being mindful that, "I am doing this just for myself", is a gift to yourself which will help to brighten your days.

Doing good things for yourself is a way of giving yourself a "hug", loving on yourself. With practice we can learn to make every day into a good day.

About the Author

Dehner Franks is a musician and author. He works as a professional pianist with the Houston Methodist Hospital in Houston, Texas as a part of their Arts in Medicine integration program. Additionally, he and his wife, Jan tour together, performing concerts, both nationally and internationally, featuring a variety of vocal and instrumental musical styles.

Franks is a composer/lyricist and a published author, having written other self-help books and original plays and musicals. He is the author of the book, Accessing My Inheritance.

Dehner has a love of people and through his work shares his music and his ideas with others freely. He has served as a minister in church ministries in Seattle, Las Vegas, and in Houston.

He currently resides in Houston, Texas with his wife who is also a poet, musician and author. Together he and Jan use their music and their teachings to motivate and to inspire others.

References

Aurelius, M. (121 AD - 180 ADa). *Happiness of your life*

Aurelius, M. (121 AD - 180 ADb). *Our thoughts*

Bonapart, N. (1823). *Imagination rules the world*. Saint Helena:

Brown, L. *Don't let someone else's opinion of you become your reality*. Unpublished manuscript. Retrieved from Brainyquote.com/quotes/les_brown.32878

Carnegie, D. (1955). *Steps to success*

Chicago Tribune. (1985, January 20,). The Body Pharmacy. *Chicago Tribune* Retrieved from chicagotribune.com

Chopra, D. (1993a). *Ageless Body Timeless Mind --- placebo effect cont....* (First Edition ed.) Harmony.

Chopra, D. (1993b). *Ageless Body Timeless Mind* (First Edition ed.) Harmony.

Chopra, D. (1993c). *Aging* (First Edition ed.) Harmony.

Chopra, D. (1993d). *Aging continued...* (First Edition ed.) Harmony.

Chopra, D. (1993e). *Mind-body connection in medicine* (First Edition ed.) Harmony. Netflix (Producer), & Dan Buettner (Director). (2023). *Live to 100: Secrets of the Blue Zones.* [Video/DVD]

Duff, G. (2023). Remembering Longtime Seattle Business Leader George Duff. *Seattle Times*, Renata Geraldo,

Dyer, W. W. (2015). *State of mind*

Einstein, A. (a). *Imagination is everything*

Einstein, A. (b). *Invisible piper*

Einstein, A. (c). *Match the frequency*

Einstein, A. (d). *Vastness of the universe*

Einstein, A. (1929, 26 October). Imagination is more important than knowledge. *What Life Means to Einstein: An Interview* by George Sylvester Viereck, Emerson, R. W. (1882). *The universe conspires*

Gandhi, M. (a). *Infinite creativity*

Gandhi, M. (b). Serving others.

Gandhi, M. (1948). *Gandhi quote*

Hammerstein II, O., & Rogers, R. (1959). *A bell's not a bell 'til you ring it...* Rogers and Hammerstein.

It Takes Will - Memoirs by Will Smith (2021). Penguin Press.

James, W. (1910). *Change your life*

Jampolsky, G. G. (1979). *Love is Letting Go of Fear* (1st ed.). Berkeley, CA: Celestial Arts.

Jordan, M., & Zorn, E. (1997, May 19,). Without Failure Jordan Would be False Idol. Retrieved from www.chicagotribune.com

Laurens Van Der Post. (1993). *A Far Off Place* - Walt Disney Pictures, Amblin Entertainment, Touchwood Pacific Partners.

Mandela, N. (2022). Forgiveness. Retrieved from www.vaticannews.va

Mandela, N., & Gisotti, A. (2022). Forgiveness will liberate you. Retrieved from www.vaticannews.va

Pasteur, L. (December 7, 1854). *Louis Pasteur: Chance favors the prepared mind.*

W.P. Kinsella; *The Field of Dreams.* Robinson, P. A. (Director). (1989). [Motion Picture] USA: Universal Studios.

Rohn, J. (2009a). *Formal education vs self education*

Rohn, J. (2009b). *Give the gift of your attention*

Rohn, J. (2009c). *Success*

Segal, I. (2010). *The Secret Language of Your Body: The essential guide to health and wellness*

Shakespeare, W. (1616). *The fault, dear Brutus...*

Singer, M. A. (2007). *Untethered soul*

Tan, C. (2012). *Search Inside Yourself: The unexpected path to achieving success, happiness (and world peace)* (First Edition ed.). http://www.harpercollins. com: Harper Collins Publishers.

Tan, C. (2013). *Search inside yourself: The unexpected path to achieving success, happiness* (and world peace)

Tesla, N. (1943). *Secrets of the universe*

Visualization works (1995). (B. Walters Trans.). The Barbara Walters Show.

Washington, M. (1802). *Cheerful and happy*

Winfrey, O. (a). *Helping others*

Winfrey, O. (b). *The mind connectory*

Winfrey, O. (c). *Your wildest dreams.* `:

Winfrey, O. (2016). *Oprah quote*

Winfrey, O. (2021). *Oprah quote*